Be the
Rooster

A PRACTICAL GUIDE TO SURVIVING
IN CORPORATE MANAGEMENT

Robert Schulman

ISBN: 1463582420
ISBN 13: 9781463582425

Library of Congress Control Number: 2011909938
CreateSpace, North Charleston, SC

Table of Contents

Table of Contents

Introduction

TODAY'S BUSINESS ENVIRONMENT

*"No battle [business] plan survives contact
with the enemy."*
—Field Marshall Helmuth Karl
Bernhard von Moltke

B usiness is war. Let me be clear: there are real winners and real losers. The winners get rich and famous, and the losers *die*. In a bad business environment with stagnant wages and high unemployment like the current mess in this country, if you run with the herd, you end up a lamb chop. John P. Getty once said, "The meek shall inherit the earth, but not the mineral rights." He meant it!

The current environment is lousy. Most of you wish that you had picked a different line of work and believe, rationally or otherwise, that everybody else has it easier. It has never been any easier; business, by its nature, is supposed to be hard. The system has evolved to weed out the losers and over reward the winners. Let me remind you that you likely selected business to earn an above-average income. I have just entered my sixth decade of working, but I am not

1

quite as old as I sound. I started working in the late sixties and have worked in each decade since. I even claim credit for the 2010 to 2020 decade; in my mind, part-time consultant and author counts. My work experience is mostly in financial services, where I have done just about everything, including taking out the trash.

The nature of financial services has forced me to spend time understanding how a variety of businesses operate. I have served on the operating committees and boards of numerous other business ventures. I have been involved with companies that make actual "stuff." I have even built a public company from scratch. I sold it to a larger company, got paid, and got out of town before the business blew up.

The business environment will change—it is always changing, and there is no reason to expect anything different going forward. The certainty of a changing business environment is the only thing you can actually depend upon. That inevitable change, properly understood, is often visible and predictable and therefore creates opportunity. Yet that realization comes as a surprise to most because there is a strong, natural and stupid presumption that what is shall continue to be for the foreseeable future. This irrational belief suggests that we should rely on the past to predict the future. The future will be different from the past, that being said it should not suggest to you that the past will repeat if you just wait long enough. Recently, President Obama was set to be reelected because he had killed Osama bin Laden. Even more recently, however, he was certain to lose because of bad economic reports. Everyone's focus has shortened materially.

Conventional wisdom suggests that people like to invest in things that are popular and are therefore over-priced. The nature of all capital assets is that as they become more popular, their value increases. Every empirical study suggests that contrary behavior is a more profitable approach to making money. The recent past is in no way predictive of short-term future outcomes. In some studies of random events like coin flips and roulette wheel spins, researchers have found no relationship between past and future outcomes. If three coin flips in a row come up heads, there is still a 50 percent chance that the next outcome will be heads. Each outcome is independent of every other out-come. In real estate, stocks, or any other capital asset, how-ever, the outcomes *are* dependent upon the past. Studies strongly suggest that good outcomes are useful predictors of future bad outcomes. Unfortunately, people tend to use past good outcomes to predict future good outcomes. This is perfectly understandable human behavior, but it can often lead to disaster.

For example, in 2007, what I call *FOOLS*—"followers over obvious ledges"—were making millions by borrow-ing money and buying Florida condos, only to resell them a few short months later at higher prices before ever taking delivery. Brilliant banks aided these *FOOLS* by making 100 percent loans to facilitate the purchase of these "foolproof" condos. The bubble was in front of everyone's face. It had every classic symptom: there was rampant overbuilding, prices were rising faster than incomes, buyers were unsophisticated, there was excess leverage, and investors had a Godlike belief that real estate prices could go nowhere but up. In fact, with no scope of history and even less common sense, a cult of thirty-five-and-under "experts" developed, explaining that real estate never actually declined in price. (They would have to be under thirty-five to ensure that they could not remember the last double-digit real estate price decline: from 1992 to 1994.) What do you need to wake up and smell the coffee, a message carved in stone at the top of a mountain?

Now the market has declined 50 to 70 percent, and condos are selling well below the cost of replacement. The *FOOLS* are broke. They have lost everything, and they will not be players in the future recovery. The smart money is not protected from stupid thinking: they are suffering from the fear of the repeat of the most recent past. Therefore they are frozen: unwilling to take advantage, of what may now be, very attractive prices. Time will pass, change will continue, the smart investors will drip in and buy a little, the market will stabilize, and more smart investors will begin to pour money into the busted condo market. Prices will begin to rise. Semi-smart investors will get worried about missing the bottom. Greed will seize control, replacing fear as the prime motivator of behavior. This greed will drive prices higher for months, maybe years. The buyer, as the rally continues, will become ever less sophisticated. In the end, at some unpredictable point down the road after the prices have reached new highs, *FOOLS* will again rush in at the top of the cycle, just like the last time, buying property from smart buyers who are now selling. The *FOOLS* will be hell-bent on disposing of any cash they might have acquired or credit they might have reestablished since the last time they were wiped out. Not surprisingly, they will be equally successful in their financial suicide mission.

In 2011 as I write this chapter, the herd, afraid of the stock market, which has had disappointing outcomes during the last eleven years, is putting record amounts of money into bond funds—just as bonds reach historically high prices and yields reach all-time lows. It will be sadly predictable how that works out for them.

It's important, early on in any discussion on the subject of business, to dissuade you of a primary business myth. Even though everybody in the business thinks that his or her business is different, in fact, all businesses are composed of virtually the same elements. People tend to view their specific business as something extraordinary. For example, the people who work in the garment business describe themselves as the craziest, drunkest, horniest, and wildest people. What they really mean is that the most successful people in their field of business—a group in which they invariably include themselves—are the smartest, most intense, most fun-loving, highest-paid, and honest people in any business. When I coach executives, they describe folks *not* in their business as "civilians"—implying that civilians are incapable of appreciating the complex nuances, challenges, and opportunities of their "very unique" business. At the risk of bursting these executives' bubbles, the fact is that the risks, challenges, and opportunities are largely the same in all human social constructs. So what contributes to the success of any business? It's simple: understand what a business needs and commit to the effort. So what does a business need to succeed? In broad strokes, businesses must accomplish the following:

1. Envision and build the right products or services.
2. Distribute and support those products or services effectively.
3. Acquire and deploy capital to fund existing business and new initiatives.
4. Maintain existing business while engaging in a continuous process of improvement and innovation.
5. Hire and retain the best and brightest people who can successfully execute numbers 1 through 4.

The bedrock of your business success—your ability to accomplish steps 1 through 5—is based upon your ability to manage (chapter 1), your ability to lead (chapter 2), and your ability to negotiate internally or to sell externally (chapter 3). In this book, I intend to show you that these skills are not the same; in fact, they are quite different and often conflicting. You can be great at one and terrible at the others and still fail or succeed. History is replete with great leaders who were lousy managers (Ronald Reagan) and great managers who were lousy leaders (Jimmy Carter). Success came to one and failure to the other based on their ability to compensate for their own inadequacies. This suggests that self-awareness and flexibility may be more important than actual talent. In chapter 3, I will give you an approach to being effective in deploying the management and leadership principals we will discuss in chapters 1 and 2.

Much has been written about the Peter Principle. In summary, the principle suggests that people advance their careers until they get promoted to a job whose requirements they are unable to competently perform. At that point they are stuck in a job that they perform inadequately, they end their advancement opportunities, and they damage the organization they are employed by.

We have all seen successful businesspeople promoted to a job they cannot do. The dualism between management and leadership explains this phenomenon. As we explore each, in chapters 1 and 2, you will learn that the further you advance in management, the more predominant is the requirement for leadership skills. If you assume that climbing the corporate ladder will be easy for you, remember that only successful managers receive management promotions—but yet there is still a meaningful failure rate.

CHAPTER 1

Management

"Who says elephants can't dance?"
—Louis Gerstner, CEO of IBM,
after engineering his company's
extraordinary turnaround

SO WHAT DO YOU DO FIRST?

THE CULTURE

Create a corporate culture. It doesn't matter whether you have just been promoted for the first time and are supervising two contemporaries you worked with and went drinking with yesterday; you run a division of a company; or you are the COO of a large business. You are the chief culture officer. There is an old saying, "Lead by example." This statement, like many old sayings, is false. In fact, you may manage by example, which we will talk about in this chapter, but leadership is entirely different. (For more on leadership, see chapter 2.)

Own and speak from the moral high ground every day. There is no more trash talk about the company, the boss, the products, the sales department, or anything else. Keeping your mouth shut is harder than you might think; everybody wants to be one of the guys or one of the girls. Humans are social creatures and are very attuned to changes in their social environment. Getting promoted may cost you friends and a social life. Haven't you already experienced this? Your friend Sue, at work, receives a promotion to manager. Suddenly she is less available and there are topics she will no longer discuss. The nature and depth of your relationship with your new manager has changed. Somewhere down the line someone asks you, "Why is Sue acting differently?" And you tell them, "Her promotion went to her head. She's filled with a sense of self-importance. You can't even make a joke about the company when she's around. She's the one who used to talk about Bob's bad social skills or Barbara's great body, but look at her now: she is really a sellout."

But let's look at what is really going on. Sue is toeing the company line. She has left the role of worker and entered the lonely tunnel called management. Sue's new company friends will be people at her level. If history is any judge, most of her old company friends will fall by the wayside over time, often because they cannot accept the changes in Sue and the new rules of the relationship. If Sue is self-aware, she will understand the changing dynamic and will adjust her interactions. She will try to find a new but positive way to maintain these relationships. Sometimes she will be successful. More often she will fail in this endeavor.

Management may represent a greater challenge to the subset of managers whose important social interactions are often with people from work. They will suffer a greater feeling of loss and isolation then their less sensitive, more well-rounded counterparts. If you are considering a career in management, consider the changes it will require of you. This may sound like a bunch of corporate mumbo-jumbo, but you would be surprised how many people are highly dependent on their work-based social interactions—becoming a manager will change all of that. So as you consider accepting a management position, consider the effects on your social life. A level of social introspection should be integrated into your decision-making equation.

Let's cover another cultural issue up front. Never tell anyone in your organization anything confidential. A successfully kept secret between two individuals is only possible under three circumstances:

1. Both parties have as much to lose from disclosure (mutually assured destruction).
2. The secret itself is so unimportant or uninteresting to normal gossip hounds that it would not be worth disclosing.
3. *At least one of the individuals is dead.*

I will deal with back-channel bandwidth (BCB) later on in this chapter, but suffice it to say that the fastest and often the most effective way to deliver any message far and wide is to divulge it to any three people at the company in utmost confidence.

Corporate culture involves many things, including rewarding excellence, creating a meritocracy, and learning to listen without the need to respond on the fly. In short, to create a healthy corporate culture, you must wrap yourself in the corporate flag and wear it like you mean it. At first, it will feel weird—as if you just became a corporate suck-up but it is your first step in a long journey to successful manager and, ultimately, to leader. Get used to it. If you succeed, you will be a manager for the rest of your working life. If the idea of acting like a corporate person makes your skin crawl, slowly put this book back on the shelf, back away, and run out of the bookstore. I promise you I will not be insulted. Seriously, if this is not your cup of tea, consider being a great individual contributor. It is actually easier to get a good job doing what you want to do if you communicate up front that you are not interested in a management-track job.

So now you are a manager. As a manager, you should treat all employees as if they were entrepreneurs and demand from them, formally or informally, that they act as such. Your job title and scope of responsibility are not relevant. If you have your micro-culture (as described above) right, you have created an environment in which entrepreneurism can flourish. Your employees will understand that they work for the company. You have demonstrated and preached that your success—and by implication their success—comes from making the enterprise more successful.

You have helped your reports to overcome the idea that a good job is defined by what they can get away with or not do. They understand that their successes will be ascribed to them and that their failures will be, at least in part, shared by you.

This allows you to change the focus from what *you* can do to make their jobs better to how *we* can make the business better. As a manager in the twenty-first century, your most important asset is the gray matter between your employees' ears. Learn to harness these assets. Your ability to do this is the leverageable, scalable skill set that will get you promoted. As soon as you enter management, you will be judged on your success in getting your employees to do what they are expected to do better, faster, cleaner, cheaper, and of higher quality.

Sam Walton said, "The people who work here know how to do it better. We just don't know how to get them to tell us." You need to get your reports to bring you their solutions, not their complaints, because those great ideas are the key to your mutual future success in corporate life, and the ability to access them is part of what a manager is paid to do. So how do you do it? First, you tell your employees that you want them to be entrepreneurs. Then you tell them they will get the credit for it, and then you give them credit for it, which is how you build team trust. Listen instead of talking, even though talking is easier, faster, and maybe even more comfortable for you. You must abandon the idea that you know the answer and instead create an environment in which you listen—even though you think you already know the best answer. But remember, you must set the ground rules for the delivery of these ideas.

Here is the value proposition: you will listen to and actively consider every idea presented as long as it contains in every case a feasible implementation plan that includes timetables, costs, risks, benefits, and challenges. In the environment we are creating, everyone is an entrepreneur, so no one gets to complain or throw around nonexecutable, self-serving plans. More importantly, the plan should not create work for you. You are the manager. You get to ask questions. You get to ask for follow-up analysis. You leverage your time and energy. If your entrepreneurial reports are driving the creative process and they get involved in reshaping their workflow, everybody wins. You get the brass ring by managing an increasing number of complex, value-added activities. You cannot direct each employee and each implementation. In an ideal circumstance, the employees are directing you. This is why it is so important to imprint the concept of entrepreneurism into your corporate culture.

Now you have a bunch of folks who think they are Bill Gates. How do you manage the creative free-for-all? First, remember that the goal is to find and execute a few good ideas with visible benefits in which the payback is demonstrable and the risks are justified. If you get too many ideas, you have to select the best. Some ideas are just plain crazy. You are being paid for your adult judgment; use it. Some ideas are so far over-the-top that you need to kill them at inception even if they meet the other criteria for consideration. Some ideas are intriguing but too far from the mission statement of the enterprise or your scope of responsibility. They should be kept alive with continued development, but the resources devoted to them should be limited. At some point, your mission may expand or you may be able to swap the idea to the area of the firm most suited to developing it. You can often enhance your position by being a team player. Every enterprise needs a Skunk Works (a secret weapons development site in California). You can delay— put the project on next year's agenda and see if it holds up to the test of time. Worthy projects may not make the cut simply because there are inadequate resources available to undertake implementation.

If an idea is beyond the scale and scope of your job description, you have no choice but to take it upstairs. "Taking it upstairs"—as opposed to "kicking it upstairs"— means that you recommend it and give credit to the creators, but you also invite blame on yourself if they hate it upstairs. Welcome to management. You have now entered higher-risk territory. The easiest and safest thing to do is to kick it up the line: "Mary on my staff thinks this is a great idea, so I am passing it on for your consideration." Then you can blame senior management for what they did or did not do with it. You can expect, with great certainty, that any idea that goes upstairs unsponsored will be ignored and will die in obscurity. Sometimes you may be tempted to use this pocket veto to get rid of a high-risk, high-reward proposal. If you are perceived by your superiors to be gaming the corporate hierarchy, however, they may see that you are ignoring a potentially great idea. Walking away from good but high-risk opportunities is corporate code for not developing scalable skills. Timidity may limit your ability to advance in the organization. People move up because they protect their managers and their subordinates, not because they throw them under the bus at the first sign of trouble.

If you take something upstairs, you are able to practice what you preach as a manager. Bring the person who has generated the idea with you, and let him or her be present or even make the presentation. If the response is favorable, you have a chance to highlight the contribution of your staff member. If the response is negative, you can step between the staff member and senior management and take some of the heat for what senior management might view as a waste of their time. In either case, you are taking advantage of a teachable moment. You are scoring points both ways. You show your reports that you will share the credit so that their efforts are not wasted. You are also managing up effectively. If you take some of the heat for a failed presentation, you show that you are a qualified manager who is supportive of your employees' efforts to improve the enterprise. This is how you model for senior management the behavior they should use in dealing with you.

Too often, the opposite happens: the manager takes the idea to his or her boss. If the boss likes the idea, the manager claims it as his or her own. If the boss hates the idea, the manager blames the actual idea generator. If you allow your insecurity or greed for credit to take you down this road, you are sowing the seeds of your own failure as a manager. Remember, *there are no secrets*. Everyone will eventually figure out what has happened, especially if this is part of your normal operating procedure. Neither your employees nor your superiors will trust you, and your career in management will be on its way down the drain.

It is impossible to overestimate the importance of not appearing insecure. You cannot bury your employees to make yourself look good. I understand that there is insecurity in each of us that may make us think, "I don't want Joe to look that good—he'll become a threat to me." Fight that reaction and make the leap of faith that your path to success is built on the quality of your employees' performance. Coach a team, go to a shrink, but keep it under control.

Creating this corporate culture requires a balance between the broad conceptualization of a philosophy and a set of clear, understandable directions. The younger and more inexperienced your reports, the more direct your instructions to them regarding their behavior must be. Twentysomethings are fresh out of school, and many do not connect their behavior with corporate goals. They are used to life being about them, and they have not made the transformation from learning to contributing. Not surprisingly, they are focused on themselves. They are infected by the success of their cohorts in their thirties. Fifteen years ago, in many professions, qualified workers had jobs thrown at them after they completed their education and found themselves deciding between multiple good offers. The focus of the employee was on having fun and learning a lot at their job so they would be prepared for the next great job. I hope anyone reading this book already understands that the current environment is quite different. It may be a long time before the pendulum swings back. So how do we deliver the cultural message to the newbie? Let us start simply. Give them a list of things you never want to hear:

It is not my job.
It is too easy, too hard, or too boring.
There is only one way to do this.
It is someone else's fault (named or unnamed).
I want to tell you something in complete confidence.

This is a sample list and is by no means complete. Create your own list; your employees will give you plenty of additional thoughts. Do not be afraid to share your list and tell your direct reports up front, the work lifestyle you want. Do not be afraid to communicate that there are other places they could work where less might be expected of them, and they are always free to look there for their next job.

As a side note, the reason someone cannot speak to you in complete confidence is that you are duty bound to break your promise under many circumstances. You are a manager. Your loyalty belongs to the name on the bottom of your paycheck. Almost anything that your employee tells you is going to create a conflict and force you into decisions that you do not want to make. Many things shared by coworkers can create conflicts for you as a manager. Some quick examples include the following: "My wife is pregnant, and I plan to quit and stay home," "I have a new job starting in a month," "I know that Joan takes money from petty cash,"

"Phil lies on his time card," and "Sally is sleeping with Harry even though she reports to him." The list of possible secrets you do not want to know could fill its own book.

Beware of the dreaded back channel. The back-channel bandwidth is at least twice the bandwidth of the front channel. The front channel includes the sum total of all the formal ways an organization communicates to its employees and other stakeholders. The back channel is all other forms of communication. People derive power and inclusion from sharing nonpublic information. Everyone has had the experience of having some personal matter exposed; most of us have both suffered from it and been guilty of inappropriate sharing. The proliferation of cell phones, texting, e-mail, and tweets has increased the speed and dependability of gossip. It has also rendered gossip less personal and therefore easier to rationalize. Business environments, like families, are filled with secret connections. A majority of those connections will not be visible to you. Trusting that nonpublic information will stay that way because your team is loyal and professional is naive. If you still think you can trust your employees to keep their mouths shut, Google "Landmark Bridges for Sale" and follow the directions exactly.

Despite all this, the workplace does not need to be a dreary place. Bring your interests to bear. Nothing I have said suggests that work can't be fun. If you have a sense of humor, don't be afraid to use it. If you share a common interest (i.e., sports, fashion, TV, movies, or the stock market) with your reports, talk about it. Stay away from politics, religion, child rearing, and the like. Think about hard work as a social activity that you can participate in together. It can be a friendly competition, with small prizes and special recognitions. Some of this may seem bush league, but remember, we are trying to build a culture of hard work, friendly competition, and social interaction. This is not a bad place to start.

Pace yourself. This is a marathon, not a sprint. If your long-term career plan is to remain in management and someday start, run, or take over an enterprise, these behaviors need to become second nature and feel natural. Trust me when I tell you that you cannot work for forty years, or even twenty, by putting on an act every day. The stress will kill you or poison the rest of your life. If you want to stay in management, develop your skills so that you can, ultimately, lead. You need to own your behavior. Let it permeate your business demeanor. Abandon cynicism, negativism, and unrestrained collegial behavior. Expect to feel optimistic and a little bit lonely, and embrace the role of being a company person. That is what is expected of you, and it is a subjective—but rather significant—measurement of your performance.

THE CHALLENGE

Well, all this certainly sounds easy...yeah, right! Let's remember that extraordinary creativity is required to envision a successful product or service. To get it right, everyone needs to be involved. Young people are often more creative than their older managers. Their input is valuable, but everyone needs to be inculcated into the culture that ideas need and deserve mini–business plans, including costs, risks, timelines, and an understanding of missed opportunities represented by the untaken paths.

The world is moving so rapidly that the marketing and sales of new ideas come with increasing speed and greater complexity. As a product purveyor, you must correctly guess who is going to buy the product. Twenty-five-year-olds experience what to buy and how to buy it using entirely different tools than their forty-five- or sixty-five-year-old counterparts. Some managers have argued, persuasively, that marketing managers should be the age of their target market; the theory suggests that only a twenty-five-year-old has experienced the world like other twenty-five-year-olds You may not be able to use social networking for the over-fifty crowd. If you text instead of tweet, you may turn off the under-twenty-five crowd. Please remember: "No battle [or business] plan ever survives contact with the enemy [customer/client]." You must always be willing to embrace change. No one ever remembers what the original plan was if the final plan succeeds. If it fails, everyone remembers how much the plan cost, whose idea it was, and how long it took.

It will take the actionable input of your entire organization to survive the business wars. In business, unless you have reached too-big-to-fail status, there are winners and losers. I have attempted to bring some humor to this book so that it does not put you to sleep, but corporate success is a deadly serious business. If you get it wrong, your company dies, the stockholders lose everything, and the employees lose their jobs. Change has become an essential ingredient in continued growth at successful enterprises. Consider a company like IBM that has been successful since the fifties. It has reinvented itself from top to bottom—twice—to continue winning the corporate wars. On the other hand, look at General Motors, which failed to take risks and innovate and has taken itself to the precipice of bankruptcy. (It has gotten off the ledge for the moment, but only with the government's intervention.) As you build your career, you will be judged by the success or failure of the enterprises for which you have responsibility. Their failures will rarely enhance your future employment opportunities.

EVOLVE YOUR ORGANIZATION

Congratulations! You have taken the first steps toward building your corporate culture. You have implemented a plan based on respect for the organization, open communication, responsibility in the form of credit, and blame for failure of decision- making. You have a realistic understanding of the challenges. Now let us get to work on organization. I have used the word *evolve* rather than *create*. Management textbooks are easy to write, but dealing with real human issues is a much more complex challenge. As you enter a new job with new responsibilities, either within your existing firm or at a new employer, you will find you have three types of employees: great employees doing what they should be doing, good employees in the wrong jobs, and undesirable employees—whom you either can or cannot dismiss on the spot. *Stop!* Take a minimum of two weeks before you do anything. Ignore the earlier general advice in this book and, for the first two weeks, accept confidential, nonpersonal information from any employee willing to share his or her vision. Give your new employees a one-time, no-risk opportunity to tell you how they would construct an organization. Listen and say nothing. You will hear many things you do not agree with, plenty of ideas that make no executable sense, and some plans that are transparently self-serving, but you will also hear some common themes. These themes may or may not influence your final judgments, but they will help you frame your thinking.

The following statement will be the most difficult for you to accept: You have meaningful weaknesses in your skills and predisposition that will damage your future success. Let me prove it to you. Play this little game with me. You walk in Monday morning and find that the wind has blown all the tasks you need to complete this week into a jumble in the middle of your desk. They include the following: scheduling and giving performance reviews to several employees, interviewing job applicants, firing an employee with whom you once had a personal relationship, setting up and attending a new product development meeting, chairing the operational review committee to review detailed operational procedures, calling clients to give good news, calling clients to give bad news that may result in losing the clients, meeting with HR to discuss fire drill safety, wishing your assistant a happy birthday, and reviewing your budget line by line in a three-hour meeting with three accountants from the CFO's office.

Take a minute before reading on. Think of how you will handle this challenge. To add one more challenge, your boss walks by at that very moment. He is familiar with your task list and says, "Organize it any way you please because everything on your list is of equal importance." So how do you handle this? In what order will you perform your tasks? Are you ready for the answer? There is only one correct answer: Pick up the first piece of paper, at random, and do it; then the next, until you reach the bottom of the pile. We have defined the tasks as equally important, yet you likely define your bias by the order in which you choose to do them. We all like to do some things more than other things; we all believe that we are better at some things than others. It is a short leap from there to elevating the things we like or do well and marginalizing the things we do less well or hate doing. That is fine in a recreational venue but potentially destructive in a corporate setting. Yes, you really have weaknesses. If you do not know what they are, you need to find out. If you are sure you have no weaknesses, you have a communication problem with yourself. You need to address this issue if you are serious about management.

Do a 360 on yourself in front of a mirror. A typical 360 is a full turn—a questionnaire, completed anonymously, by people you work with. HR has them, or you can get one online if need be. This assessment will allow you to find out how people view your skills—not only your reports but also your coworkers and your superiors. A debrief with your reports will allow you to understand their view of your management weaknesses, or "areas to be strengthened," if it makes you feel better. It will empower your reports to hold you accountable for the behaviors you agree to work on modifying. I am certain that you will find the exercise humbling and instructive. You must understand how you are perceived. That does not mean that you need to correct all the behaviors that your reports do not like. You may in fact be very comfortable with behaviors that make them uncomfortable. This is about communication; it is not about handing the inmates the keys to the asylum. I cannot over-state the importance of gaining this insight. Perception is reality. How you are viewed is an extraordinary tool in understanding your coworkers' interactions with you.

The leap you must make is in learning to value skills sets that you don't like or are not good at equally with your strong areas. The inability of corporate America to appre-ciate differences may even have contributed to the melt-down of 2008. Every specialty thinks its contribution is the most important. Ask a salesperson what he thinks of client service or marketing. You will likely get an earful on how he could be paid better if the firm didn't waste money on silly stuff like branding or advertising. Marketing will tell you that the sales department is overpaid, that salespeople bring no real skills to their job, and that they don't pull their own weight. The truth is, a successful business needs every specialty doing its job.

Surround yourself with people who are strong where you are weak or disinterested. Hold all skill sets in high esteem. Pay people competitively. Begin to deal with your silo issues up front. Do not bad-mouth accounting or any other department. Nobody gets to blame his or her failures on some other team. That is the easy way, but it is not the smart way. That kind of behavior is visible organizationally, and the favor is generally returned at a really bad time in your career path. I know I am ruining all your fun by warning you off all these easy and fun approaches to management. You want fun—go to the beach. You want success—do it the hard way.

Unless you are an organizational superstar (and I will tell you up front I am not), beg, borrow, steal, or hire an organizational superstar, someone who loves it; someone who eats, breathes, and lives details; someone who likes his or her paper clips in alphabetical order. Don't hire a recent B-school graduate who really wants to be an investment banker. Project and finance management are essential for any enterprise. Your success is dependent, in part, on how well you understand and can articulate exactly what is going on in your business. Your superstar is the key ingredient in the creation of that articulation. Your organizational person should be loyal to a fault and should nit-pick you and everyone else until you want to scream.

Seek a lawyer, or the use of one, who has a business brain. Lawyers who work in a corporate environment understand that they will stay employed longer if, when in any doubt, they say no. Lawyers are not rewarded for a venture's success, but they are fired if they get it wrong. An activity that has a ten percent chance of being illegal may be an acceptable "business risk" to you. The lawyer views that ten percent risk as a career ender. You are paid to take risks and guess correctly most of the time. She is paid to prevent ille-gal activity irrespective of the magnitude of the business opportunity. Your lawyer should be induced and encour-aged to act like a businessperson. She needs to adjust her perspective from "Is it legal?" to "How do we accomplish this in a legal fashion?" Not all lawyers are willing to adopt this mindset. It is more comfortable to say yes or no than to be creative and to evaluate rational business risks. If you find a lawyer that can get her head into the business game, do everything you can to work with her.

I mentioned silos earlier, and we will deal with them in detail later on, but you need context for the term. A *silo* is the structure that all managers seek to create around their area of responsibility. It involves creating a closed system where all of the resources necessary to perform the assigned func-tion report to the manager. A silo represents a closed sys-tem of management. All or many of the required resources are inside the silo; it has its own marketing, sales, client services, even its own lawyers and accountants. Managers like this system because they are in control of their environ-ment. They have lots of levers to pull and buttons to press. It makes them feel important and powerful. Because of this, the "cone of silence" is employed: What goes on in the silo stays in the silo; don't go cooperating with outsiders from other parts of the firm who want to find out what we are up to. There are clear positives and negatives to the silo system, which we will discuss further.

You must overcome the bias of your background: assume that all the pieces it takes to run a firm are equally important. We all come from some background in business. We all speak a "first language" that we developed when we entered the business world. The most common error businesspeople make is to surround themselves with people who have similar backgrounds and employment histories. Engineers love other engineers, and salespeople think that how you sell is more important than what you sell. This arrogance continues throughout the disciplines. The numbers guys (or gals) think that if reporting is great a business will succeed. Fight past this ideology. Hire and promote people who do not share your vision on how to accomplish the firm's goals but who can and do embrace, with great clarity, your vision of what those goals should be.

So you have gotten started. Leave your great employees in place and give them additional responsibilities. Meet with them to tell them how impressed you are with what they have accomplished and how confident you are that they will continue to be successful with their new responsibilities. Move your good but underperforming employees to areas that better fit their skills sets. Encourage your employees to relax and get back to work (everyone hates and fears change), and assure them that they have a career opportunity in your group. Get rid of the real underperforming employees—or at least reposition them to neutralize their negative influence as much as possible.

Ah, if only it were that easy. We will cover employee types and tools to deal with each type later in this chapter. Getting the right people in the right jobs for the right compensation is a big part of why the company is paying you. Not all employees are created equal. To create a fair corporate culture and operate a meritocracy, I outlined at the beginning of this chapter a set of rules that need to be applied fairly to all employees. Even so, you do not have the luxury of managing everyone using the same methods. If we could do that effectively, we would be able to handle many more direct reports, and this book could be even more succinct. Common belief in management-speak is that seven to ten direct reports is all any manager should have. My experience suggests those numbers are correct. If you find yourself suffering from report creep, consider a reorganization that allows you to create a new more stream-lined structure. That will free up the time for you to focus on your best people.

EXECUTION IS EVERYTHING

Schedule a weekly staff meeting. I suggest Monday morn-ing—as early as your industry will tolerate. Make sure every-one understands it is his or her job to attend. For ninety minutes, once a week, everyone is equal. Everyone gets five to ten minutes to report on his or her plans and accomplish-ments. As the manager, you get to put a frame around the information and create a firm context around the updates. You also create a professional environment. You ask your reports to share with their counterparts what they are doing and why they are doing it. It is also your chance to share with them what is going on upstairs.

These meetings are hard to commit to. In the late eight-ies, I reported to Joe Plumeri. Joe is now the CEO of the

Willis Group (NYSE). He started me on this path of embracing staff meetings in this very ritualistic way. When I joined the firm, having been a superstar in my former firm without working hard or in a structured fashion, I told him I was too busy to attend. He told me flat out, "I understand completely. Please feel free to skip them on any Monday the stock market is closed, and be on time for the replacement meeting held Tuesday at eight a.m." As a fair alternative, I was free to resign on the spot! I never missed another staff meeting.

Management is challenging because people are not fully predictable. We have spent a lot of time talking about the rules of management. You are writing your own rules everyday as you manage your universe. You may not be aware of it, but you are processing everything you do and factoring into your future thinking how well it works. You do this to develop a road map for your behavior and managerial style. We all do this unconsciously, but we may be unable to articulate exactly what we do or why we do it. Good managers might tell you they are using their instinct. My observation is that they are accessing their well-processed experiences, not some instinctual gift.

To complicate the task even more and to illustrate the challenges of management, you must learn to manage people who need to be managed uniquely relating to their personality types, as well as according to the specific type of activity in which they are engaged. The complexity of this challenge is difficult to put into words. Fortunately, your instinct or well-processed experience will guide you as it becomes more fully developed.

BEHAVIOR

Let us talk more about behavior. There is an old parable about the turtle and the scorpion. A turtle is standing at the edge of a rapidly moving river. A scorpion approaches him and says, "Mr. Turtle, would you take me across the river on your back? I am unable to swim, and I need to get to the other side."

The turtle responds, "That would be crazy. You are a scorpion. If I expose my neck, you will sting me, and I will die."

The scorpion responds, "That would not be the case, because if you drown, I would drown as well."

The turtle, swayed by the logic of the request, agrees. The scorpion jumps on the turtle's back, and they proceed to swim across the river. As they reach the midpoint of the river, the scorpion stings the turtle on the neck. Feeling the poison working through his body and knowing that death is imminent, the turtle looks back at the scorpion and asks, "Why did you do that, knowing we will both die?"

The scorpion responds calmly, "It is just my nature."

I love animal parables and use them all the time in my management activities. I find them instructive and easy to remember, but let us remember their limitations in human analysis. They have broad application to behavior relating to a task or type of task that you may assign someone to complete. They generally do not apply to a person, only the person's behavior when faced with particular types of

challenges. Almost nobody is a pure scorpion or a pure turtle. He or she just acts like one as it relates to a specific range
of activities.

For example, take Bob, your best salesperson. He leads
your sales team and takes an active role in sales training. He,
of course, believes that making the sale is the most important element in any decision you as the manager must
make: if you are a carpenter, every job requires a hammer
and nails. You ask Bob to serve on a committee to examine
new initiatives. You do this to broaden his perspective and
give him a more general vision of the operation of the firm.
You hope that, at some point, he will develop more appli-
cable management skills that will allow him to contribute
more fully. However, Bob becomes a situational scorpion.
He uses his outgoing personality and persuasive manner to
kill every idea that comes to the committee. The more risk
he perceives to the influence of the sales areas of the firm,
the more he digs into his objections. Bob is drowning himself to protect the status quo and his short-term compensation concerns. Bob is destroying his career, either because
he cannot embrace change or because his competitive
nature wants to deny success to other areas of the firm.
This destructive behavior is a big part of American corporate culture. It may well explain why large firms often reach
a tipping point at which they become too large and diverse
to grow organically. As manager, your job is not to reinvent
Bob but to repurpose him; you have found his inner scorpion. He is comfortable selling and teaching others to sell.
He has proven that he cannot control his discomfort with

being out of a sales role. Many effective salespeople never leave sales. In fact, many effective employees cannot transition successfully to other disciplines within the organization. It's part of why many managers fail at their new jobs.

Now consider Laura, who is a perfect turtle when it comes to her job. She will generally do exactly what is asked of her, and she will complete tasks in the time allocated, but she never sees the big picture. As a result, she never has suggestions on improving performance. She is unlikely to suggest new ideas and is much more likely to seek guidance as to methodology or prioritization. Turtles generally bring good humor and stability to an organization. Unless you can find an area in which Laura does not act like a turtle, it is unlikely she has a future in management. That does not mean she has no place in the organization. She is, in fact, easy to manage, and you need people who can put their heads down and do the work. Turtles do what they are told and normally in good spirit. They are the glue that holds many organizations together.

There are also unusual animals called armadillos (also known as RITRs, or "rock in the road-ers"). They are blended creatures who are aggravating and essential to the operation of an enterprise. They have many of the elements of turtles, but they are much more valuable. They set the tone for change. They are the noncreative, superdisciplined, and detail-oriented individuals who are always asking, "but what if…" Their glass is always half empty. They have a list of concerns, which I consider rocks in the road. The armadillo is always in the rooster's way. RITRs have a list of steps and concerns that need to be checked off or solved before they will get out of the way and let the process proceed. There is no management shortcut with the armadillos. They will not sign off until you move every rock. They want a solution to every problem they can perceive before they start the implementation of any product, process, or policy. In my experience, you would be wise to listen carefully to what they are worried about. My approach is to invest the time to move every rock. My career has been bailed out more times than I can count by a smart and insightful RITR.

To understand a different type of employee, consider the story about the mule. The mule represents your most common issue as a manager. Farmer Joe is visiting Phil the farmer on Phil's farm. Phil says to Joe, "Have I told you about the special new mule I have acquired?" Joe says, "No." They head out to the barn so that Phil can show off his new mule. Phil says, to an ordinary-looking mule, "Count to ten!" The mule stamps his right front hoof ten times. Phil says, "Plow the lower forty." The mule runs over to the harness area, puts the harness on, bends his back legs to keep the plow out of the ground, runs up, and starts plowing the lower forty. The mule does the work quickly and well. The mule returns to the barn and slips the harness off. Phil says, "Relax. That's it for today." The mule trots over, turns the water supply on with his teeth, grabs a quick shower, drags a bale of hay into his stall, and relaxes for the evening.

Joe is blown away. He knows that Phil is retiring next year, and Joe is desperate to have this wonder-mule. Phil agrees to sell the mule to Joe, who loads the mule onto the back of his truck and drives home. Joe pulls up in front of his barn and instructs the mule to step off the truck and go into the barn. The mule just looks at him with a blank expression. He pulls the mule down off the truck and tries a simpler command: "Count to ten!" All he gets is another dumb look. He tries three more times and realizes Phil has taken him. So he drags the mule onto the truck and drives back to Phil's to recover his money.

When Joe returns, Phil is shocked. He walks up to the mule and says, "Count to ten!" The mule gives him a dumb look. Phil thinks for a second, picks up a five-foot length of two-by-four, and smacks the mule with it right between the eyes. Phil says, "Try it now."

The mule does everything that Joe commands, with precision. Joe asks, "What happened?"

Phil responds, "He knows what to do—*you just have to get his attention.*"

The mule represents your passive-aggressive employee; he or she can drive you crazy. As with all behaviors, acting passive-aggressive can be systemic and can apply to every aspect of a person's work life, or it can be related to specific activities. Either way, it is tough to take; no one wants to face an angry, sullen, secretive, uncommunicative employee. I have had managers who refuse to manage. They are good at completing tasks, and they are great individual contributors. Even so, something in their psychological makeup stops them from confronting others in a supervisory role. As you manage, you will discover that most employees have a "monster in the closet." There are responsibilities that will bring out the worst in someone, which can often take the form of passive-aggressive behavior that drives everyone crazy.

When you give a new responsibility to someone, he may hit the wall. This employee just cannot motivate himself to embrace the new responsibility positively. This employee has "muled out," or become passive-aggressive; in general, he has frozen in place. Some options you can consider: coaching and counseling. Sometimes something as simple as a direct discussion in which the mule can acknowledge his issues may be sufficient to break the logjam in his head. If these steps do not improve the employee's behavior as it relates to the task at hand, it is time to get your two-by-four. A forthright explanation of the career limitation the employee is placing on himself may lead to a stronger effort to control his negativism. As a last resort, you must decide if this employee is on his way to systemic mule status (which means he should be on his way to the door) or just needs a change in career direction to express his potential fully.

Situational mules must be distinguished from systemic mules. Situational mule behavior is common and often easy to remediate. As we have discussed, people hate change and tend to freak out when confronted with the need to embrace it. Systemic mules are mercifully rare. They are employees who are negative about everything. They are intensively toxic influences on the environment in which they work. They are normally fixtures in their jobs. They believe and preach that all change is bad. To make matters worse, they normally perform their jobs well and are often underpaid for their responsibilities.

They have been passed over for promotion any number of times—hence the underpaid and overqualified conundrum. Despite the challenge, these are people you must fix or fire. Janine is your classic systemic mule. She has done the same job for many years and hates change of any kind. Despite the challenges of working with her and the understandable desire to be rid of her, there is the realistic fear that Janine knows something that she has not shared. Her leaving may cause a real problem.

Systemic mules are very secretive. No matter how many times you ask, you will never get a comprehensive job description. To take action, there are also rationalizations you must overcome, which include the following: "If it's not broken, don't fix it," and "It's the dead wood that holds up the tree."

Dealing with systemic mules is a three-part process: first, embrace that the negativism is so toxic that it trumps the temptation to do nothing; next, communicate directly with Janine about what the problem is and what it would take to fix it (this is symbolically hitting her between the eyes with the two-by-four); last, prepare, in very short order, to pull the trigger.

If you couldn't tell from my comments, my experience suggests that you can usually deal with situational mules in a constructive way. On the other hand, folks who demonstrate consistent, systemic negative and passive-aggressive behavior need to be purged actively from the organization—after they have been given a fair opportunity to modify their demeanor. Although I believe it is normally beyond the scope of management to create adequate incentives for a person to abandon a well-entrenched and pervasive personality trait, that does not free us of our responsibility, as managers, to encourage the required behavioral change. Experience leaves me with little hope of success, but clear communication on this difficult subject is still essential.

Another type of employee can be seen in my favorite story. Farmer Joan is running an egg farm. Her rooster dies suddenly. You cannot run an egg farm for long without a productive rooster, so Joan gets into her truck and heads into town to fix her problem. In the general store in town, the roosters are in cages lined up on the floor on the far right. Joan walks down the aisle, looking at the roosters: Long Island Red—$55, New England Breeder—$65, Nebraska Special—$60, and the other regular breeders at similar prices. The last cage, at the back of the store, is 50 percent bigger, and the rooster in it is almost twice the normal size. The label reads, "Super Rooster—$125." Joan says to Arnie, who is behind the counter, "That's crazy! Who would ever pay $125 for a rooster?"

Arnie answers, "Trust me, Joan, this rooster is worth every penny."

Joan wants to expand her business, and it has been a good year so far. She buys the super rooster, loads the cage onto the back of the truck, and heads back to the farm. As Joan stops in front of the chicken coop, she hears the sound of ripping metal. The super rooster rips the cage to shreds and runs into the coop. For the next thirty minutes, feathers are flying, and chickens are clucking unlike anything Joan has ever heard before. The rooster runs out of the chicken coop and into the barn. Soon, odd sounds she has never heard before are emanating from the barn. Upon entering the barn, Joan can see that the horses, cows, and pigs all have bewildered but very satisfied looks on their faces. Joan catches a glimpse of the rooster heading out the back door, back into the chicken coop. The original scene in the chicken coop is recreated, with equal feather flying, clucking, and general fanfare. Joan bars the door to the coop and blocks the rooster's path when he emerges. "You are going to be a flash in the pan. If you go at this pace, you will burn out and be dead in a day or two, which does me no good!" exclaims the exasperated Joan. Ignoring her, the rooster breaks left and jumps into the pond, chasing the ducks and wild geese. Joan has had enough for one day and retires to her home for the evening. After a restless night with all kinds of odd noises coming from outside, Joan emerges to find her worst fears have come true. In the middle of the front yard, feet up in the air with buzzards circling, is the one-day wonder rooster, dead as a doornail. (I have no idea where that expression, first used in 1350, came from, but it sounded perfect here.) Joan is furious. She stands over the dead stud and screams, "See, I warned you, and now you are dead and of no use to me!"

The rooster opens one eye halfway, looks up, and whispers, "Shhh. You want to catch a buzzard, you have to play her game."

The rooster, properly managed, is your greatest leverage as a manager. If you can create for an employee a set

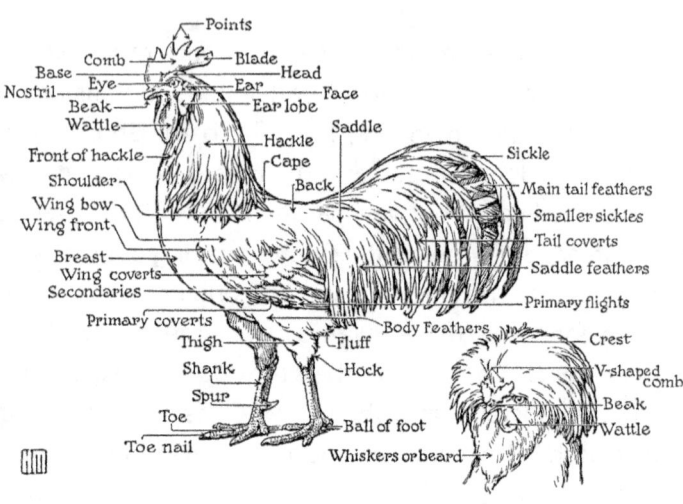

of responsibilities that allows him or her to seize the opportunity and run with it, everyone wins. Great roosters are a little scary as direct reports, but they also represent the best opportunity for you to build your career. You will have to peer into your soul and deal with your insecurities about having great employees. You get the credit, but you fear the question, "Why do we need you anymore?" This is one of the great challenges of management. How do I convince you that you should be hiring and promoting people who may be smarter, better educated, and harder working than you? Hiring roosters does create career risk. Not hiring them creates the certainty of mediocrity.

If that is not scary enough, your employees should be able to do their jobs better than you could if your situation was reversed. This may sound strange at first glance, but as a manager, you get paid to build great teams that can perform through a variety of situations, employee losses, and competitive challenges. As much as it may make you uncomfortable, you must recruit and nourish the smartest, most creative, and most motivated folks you can attract.

SPECIAL CHALLENGES

Problem employees come in various forms. We have spoken about many of them already in this chapter. There are two additional types of potential employees that I believe it would be helpful to discuss.

Let us start with the superstar. Anyone who has managed has experienced the pain and pleasure of the superstar employee. We have talked at length about building a culture and ridding our corporate world of bad influences. It is hard to fire or demote a mule who does a good job, but it is possible. The organization will back you up to let you build your team. The superstar is a different story. He or she is one of the top players in your industry. You know it, your organization knows it, and your competition knows it. The competition has tried to recruit this employee, and he works at your firm because he knows the players, or you pay the best, or you offer the most latitude in his daily life. When that changes, he is gone. There are no effective contracts; everybody is a free agent every day.

The superstar reports to you, but she built the group that she is running; you are the new player on the block. This is an uncomfortable situation. Your control is materially diminished. Let us start with the obvious: building a good relationship with this employee is integral to your success as a manager. If the superstar's reputation was built on your watch, that paints you in a great light as a developer of talent, but more likely you have been slotted in and held back so that the superstar can spend more time in her sweet spot. In extreme cases, the superstar may have been offered your job and turned it down because she likes what she is doing day-to-day better than a one-level-up management job that involves areas outside her interest. The superstar may even make as much or more money than you do.

Management is a problem-solving exercise. Every employee must be managed uniquely. That's why people write books like this one. With this "top of the heap" rooster, find out what is in his way and remove it. It may seem like menial work, but remember that the goal of management is to maximize the business outcome. (Get the rooster to the door of the hen house.) At the same time, you must make sure your contributions are visible. We are all renters of talent—the days of great contributors who stay in place are over. Most good employees seek promotions until they are engaged in something at which they are only fair. They then lose their superstar status. If they can control their ambition, they may keep the job that got them their superstar status. This creates a threat to you. They will likely cash in their chips at some point and do the job they are good at somewhere else for more money. As a manager, you are renting talent. Despite your desire to hold on to your best employees, in this environment people often leave. That is why you build real talent and redundancy into your management structures. If you have executed your mandate well, the person waiting for the vacated job is likely even better than you think.

The other type of problem employee is a bit harder to define. We have all had an employee who just has our number. There are a million reasons why that might be true, and this is not a book on self-analysis. This employee just makes you feel inadequate or uncomfortable every time you are around him. He asks for things that annoy you. You may give him what he wants so that you do not have to confront him, or you may deny his reasonable requests because you dislike him. Either way, you feel stupid, weak, or manipulated.

I am sure you all know someone like this. Seek to understand why this person is ringing your bell. Do you have trouble confronting women because they remind you of your mother? Is the employee a father figure? Do you really think these employees are smarter, do a better job, or are a threat to you in some way? Are they too old or too young? Are they too attractive or not attractive enough? You are being driven by your own insecurities! (All right, maybe this *is* a book on self-analysis.)

My problem has always been with the employee who is older than me and has been around longer than I have. If this employee is also oppositional, combative, secretive, or in any way dismissive of my suggestions, solutions, or supervision, I become crazed. They are mules, and they have my number. It has taken years for me to learn how to deal with them. My first reaction is still to run or fight, neither of which generates the outcome I am looking for. For the most part, they are valuable, smart employees, and I have a bad history of not making the best possible use of them.

The easiest approach is to fire the employee. Doing so is unfair to the employee and potentially damaging to your organization, therefore damaging to the advancement of your management career. Well-trained, productive employees are hard to come by. This is yet another instance in which management is not much fun. Be honest with yourself: if this is a bad employee, fire him or her and do not give it a second thought. More than likely, however, they are actually good employees; you owe them and your employer some self-examination. Try to define which of their behaviors are making you crazy. Accept that you need to take responsibility for your own reactions. It is incumbent on you to understand the buttons they are pushing on your psyche; a better understanding of yourself allows you to better control your reaction to their objectionable behavior.

I believe strongly in the direct approach, but it is unlikely that your employees will be able to alter their personality, age, or appearance just because it would be easier for you to deal with them if they did. Think carefully about the small changes they could make in their behavior (which they can control) that would improve your working environment. For instance, you can ask them to stop wearing purple, but you are unlikely to get them to accept that they look like a troll when they do wear it. Try anything, including professional help for yourself, to become more embracing of things that make you crazy. To quote Spider-Man's Uncle Ben, "With great power comes great responsibility."

MANAGING THE SALES CHANNEL

Managing the sales channel is a lot like virginity: it is its own punishment and its own reward. I handle this topic—the sales channel, not virginity—separately because the activity is filled with special challenges and unique opportunities. In other work specialties, you can use training and experience to build a team. When you hire a client- service specialist, you can usually attract someone by paying her more money than she currently makes, by allowing her to take on more responsibility than she had in her last position. If you have compensated these employees properly, you have enhanced the productivity of your organization and created new career paths for these employees. The same is true for accountants, lawyers, marketing people, and most other types of employees who are compensated as a function of the bottom-line outcomes of the enterprise. A combination of career factors drives most employees to make decisions, including career opportunities, financial considerations, ego gratification, the strength and prospects of the employer, and how much they like their boss and their general work environment. Successful salespeople, however, typically have different metrics for decisions. They are often driven by convenience, financial opportunity, and personal recognition. When you are selecting sales staff, successful selling experience is likely less valuable than enthusiasm, intelligence, and predisposition.

If you want to build a sales force in a hurry, the tried and true method is to go out and hire your competitor's salespeople. You do that by throwing money at them; you increase the salesperson's compensation with *no* change in his job responsibilities and expectations. Your excuse is the platitudinous bunk that you only hire the best and brightest. That, of course, is exactly what your competition is saying and doing when hiring your existing sales force. This has the highly undesirable outcome of raising sales costs and reducing overall industry productivity. Not surprisingly, the sales force and many of its leaders—who are usually former star salespeople—think this corporate suicide mission is a peachy keen idea. This insane behavior can most easily be observed in Hollywood, on Wall Street, in professional athletics, and in mental institutions. It exists in almost every industry, wrapped in industry adages like "This is the way our industry works," "Salespeople need direct motivation," and "The best situation is when salespeople eat what they kill." These rationalizations are widespread in business circles. Despite the popularity of these views, that perception is short-sighted, verging on suicidal.

Salespeople keep score mostly, but not exclusively, by cash compensation and over-stated recognition of the importance of their contributions. Everyone is interested in getting credit for what he or she does. That remains a common thread in the care and feeding of employees. In sales, employees typically expect to be paid as a function of their gross sales levels. In my experience, salespeople are usually paid—at least in part, and often predominantly—from the top-line outcomes of their efforts. Sales groups make a big deal about the importance of this practice. In reality, paying salespeople off the top tends to disconnect them from general corporate values and goals. They care about gross sales, whereas everyone else is focused on net profits.

For example, Joe (another great salesperson and a good friend of Bob, the situational scorpion from our last example) says, "If I could give a 15 percent discount to my clients, I could double my sales productivity." His logic is unassailable: "I would sell a million dollars' worth every year, instead of five hundred thousand. My sales commission at 7 percent would be seventy thousand instead of thirty-five thousand, and the company would net nine hundred thirty thousand instead of five hundred sixty-five thousand. It's a win-win all around." This makes perfect sense to Joe (anything that doubles your commission income tends to make perfect sense) and, because of Joe's top-line bias, a compelling presentation of the actual costs and outcomes to your organization would be ignored. Joe has been bred to be shortsighted; it has been ingrained in his orientation to overvalue top-line results. So what is wrong with Joe's idea?

ACTUAL OUTCOME

In a business that has a healthy 30 percent marginal profitability before sales expenses, the actual outcome would be as follows:

> Case 1: Joe sells five hundred thousand dollars' worth of your product or service.
> Three hundred and fifty thousand dollars is a variable expense.
> Thirty-five thousand dollars goes to Joe.

One hundred and fifteen thousand dollars is contribution to overhead (CTO).

Case 2: (Joe's argument) Joe sells $1.18 million worth of your product or service.

Joe gives a 15 percent discount, so the company receives a million dollars.

Eight hundred and twenty-six thousand dollars is a variable expense.

Seventy-six thousand dollars goes to Joe.

One hundred and four thousand dollars is left for CTO.

Case 3: Despite the discount, Joe only increases sales by 50 percent.

Joe sells eight hundred thousand dollars' worth of your product or service.

Joe gives a 15 percent discount and collects six hundred and eighty thousand dollars.

Five hundred and sixty thousand dollars is a variable expense.

Forty-seven thousand and six hundred dollars goes to Joe.

Seventy-two thousand and four hundred dollars is left for CTO.

Joe wins every time, yet the enterprise loses in cases 2 and 3. Joe will not find this a compelling argument. Joe has top-line bias and short-term thinking that motivates him. He is dismissive of the idea that anyone else has to receive additional payment for additional output. Organizationally, you must consider the impact of giving a discount, not only on Joe's activities, but also on your existing pricing structure and the rest of your sales effort. It is also possible that with his enhanced deal Joe may not work as hard and may fail to double his sales activities. At the end of the day, what sounds like a decent idea turns out to be a meaningful error. This oversimplified example illustrates the classic conflict of interest between sales and the rest of the organization. This conflict is a direct outgrowth of paying one type of employee on the top line and everyone else on the bottom line. When sales executives move up in management, they have to learn not to try to resolve every profit shortfall by solutions that involve the necessity to "just do more business."

When dealing with salespeople, you have less control over employee behavior. Their motivation is driven primarily by money and public recognition. Therefore, long-term, strategic decisions concerning how you will build and maintain a sales force become vitally important. You may be a manager who has never been a salesperson. Yet I believe the approach I am suggesting is equally useful. You may have been promoted through the sales channel. If you are a former salesperson, it is essential to recognize that you have a top-line bias to deal with in your decision-making. I started my life in sales, and it took me years of management experience to reign in my bias.

SO WHAT IS THE SOLUTION?
Build or buy? So now you are in charge of sales! Do not jump under the desk or out the window. We will approach this like any business challenge. The fact that you have an

existing sales force doesn't have to change the decision to buy or build. The train is moving, so you are not going to harpoon the sales process; the company needs to keep the lights on and make payroll next week. That does not mean you relegate yourself to holding on for dear life and hoping nothing goes wrong. The typical image of a sales manager reminds me of a cartoon of an elephant charging downhill (the sales force) with the manager holding onto the tail, being thrashed from side to side, and yelling, "Don't worry, I got him!"

Grab the bull by the horns, or the elephant by the trunk (I warned you, I love animal allegories), and try to freeze the existing sales force in place. Announce that there will be no change in compensation for the salespeople currently employed and that there will be a new reward in twenty-four months for sales staff still at the company. Recognition, which does cost money, is the best bang for the buck with such an incentive. Consider giving two days at a spa or a tennis or golf camp. Recognition is also psychic: if this sales group is going to be a legacy activity, titles and lots of appreciation become cheap to throw around. You can make your sales force feel central and important even though you plan for them to become an ever less important part of the future.

Your role is to put the existing sales force in a specially constructed corporate cage. You must convince the salespeople that they are lucky to be in this gilded cage. Give them titles and pats on the head and have them derive comfort from the fact that they are lucky to be there and that no new players will be included in their special deal. In other words, the deal is so great that the company is no longer willing to offer this arrangement to anyone else.

So you have dealt with the short-term concerns that your promotion or arrival has generated within the sales force. Humans hate change of any kind. They talk about change, and they embrace the idea of change until it affects them in any way. Even if they are unhappy with their existing position or circumstances, they are fearful and resistant to real change. (*Real change* is defined for this purpose as any change that might actually affect them). You need to accept that your desire to be an agent for change must be tempered with the need to keep the wheels on the train while you redecorate the dining car. I would define my approach as "Keep what you have, stop buying more of it, and build a better, cheaper, and more professional approach."

So you are on your way to two sales forces: the one you have, which it is imperative that you maintain, and the one you are going to build so that you are no longer held hostage by the one you started with. Most salespeople in American business are hired guns. They are with you because you have the easiest products to sell or you have the highest payout—or both. From the day they join you; they have one foot out the door to the next hot product offering or enriched commission structure. (This is particularly true for employees under forty who have been at your firm less than five years and have been at one or more other firms before joining yours.) Based on my experience, a majority of successful salespeople define career advancement as higher payout or better product line, as distinguished from advancement into sales management, which most of them view as a position for "losers" like you.

So how do we build a sales force? Chapter 3 is devoted to negotiation and persuasion. It is not feasible to separate negotiation and persuasion from the more specialized but essentially identical activity of sales. The twenty-first century sales employee, in my view, is becoming a corporate citizen instead of a hired gun. Many industries have seen the light and are on the road to this transition. The sales skills they need are present in a relevant number of existing and prospective employees. This is known as business development. Business development in a corporate environment is typically described as a set of activities without a clear definition. I recently tried to read a book on business development and glazed over by page ten. Wikipedia describes business development as follows:

In the field of commerce, the specialist area of business development comprises a number of techniques and responsibilities that aim at attracting new customers and penetrating existing markets.

Techniques used include:

- assessment of marketing opportunities and target markets
- intelligence gathering on customers and competitors
- generating leads for possible sales

- advising on, drafting, and enforcing sales policies and processes
- follow-up sales activity
- formal proposal and presentation management and writing
- pitch and presentation rehearsals
- business model design
- account planning and performance monitoring
- proposition development and campaign development

Business development involves evaluating a business and then realizing its full potential, using such tools as:

- marketing
- information management (sometimes conflated with knowledge management)
- customer service

In my experience, the modern approach to sales should be incorporated into the overall business development function of an organization. To do that you have to train your new sales force to play well with others. Larger firms are evolving their strategy by using sales rotations in their internship programs rather than offering a sales tract program. Almost everyone applying for a job will tell you she has a broad range of skills and interests and is looking for a broad range of possible jobs that could include pretty much *anything except sales.*

Most applicants and employees are uncomfortable with the idea of selling. They are nonconfrontational, and they are likely concerned about a variable income (i.e., the "eat what you kill" mentality). Sales is also a job where the outcomes are very visible. We talked earlier about comparing your inside feelings with everyone else's outside feelings. In a traditional sales role, everyone knows how you are performing. It is an unusual person who is comfortable naked in a room filled with people who are dressed. Sales jobs are not typically associated with career development; most people want to be part of something, not be the Lone Ranger. As a result, they shy away from the idea of a career in sales.

All of these things conspire to keep the traditional sales candidates' pool small, and therefore expensive. In the eighties, when the insurance companies and the brokerage firms studied how to hire successful salespeople, they came to some interesting and surprising conclusions. They discovered that future success as sales practitioners requires only average intelligence but a much-above-average ability to accept rejection, which is most often found in conjunction with the tendency to rationalize results by deflecting blame for unsatisfactory outcomes. "I can call the next prospect and risk rejection because it was the last prospect's fault that he didn't buy, not mine." How does this profile fit into your corporate culture? We studied this directly at EF Hutton in the late seventies. By the middle eighties it appeared the implementation of our findings had produced a measurable increase in sales productivity vis-à-vis our competitors.

So what will sales look like in the twenty-first century? Let me tell you what will not work: fast-talking, well-dressed flimflam artists who lie and promise things that cannot be delivered. I am not suggesting that there will be no more used car salespersons or vacation home consultants. I am suggesting that an increasing number of organizations are approaching sales as a problem-solving activity. I think of sales as the continuous focus on activities that motivate and inspire potential buyers to consider certain products or services and that create a sustainable set of fears concerning the risks of indecision or delay. Good examples of what we are talking about would be your experience in a corporate-owned Verizon or Apple store.

So how do you train a sales force of collaborative problem solvers? First, you must put the activity in context as part of an overall effort to deliver integrated client service, business development, marketing, and sales activities of the organization in a seamless, client-centric approach. The employee needs to be a generalist in all areas, as well as a specialist in one or more of them. The silo mentality is fatal to this effort.

Everyone in this group is responsible for sales. It is a general responsibility of the business development effort. Success is measured by the overall achievement of the group; people get bonuses, not commissions. Everyone in the group receives sales training and spends a portion of his or her time in the effort. Our mission is to get everyone on the team to focus on the goal—to inspire, motivate, and inform while creating fear in the client's mind of the potential penalty of inaction.

Effective sales training in the twenty-first century is the art of converting effective, enlightened corporate employees into effective business development officers. Yet, most corporate types cannot see themselves in sales. They may need to experience the activity firsthand. The world has changed. Marketing has gone viral; selling and closing is now part of business development. The concept of a killer presentation, which flourished in the nineties, is dead. New approaches built around team support and service have evolved.

Another area in which you can shine is in the quality of your hiring choices, as your team scale and scope grows or the current personnel move on to other places or are promoted within the organization. Actual authorization to hire is like striking corporate gold. Each selection allows you a fresh chance to bring in new ideas and to acquire skill sets otherwise not available to you. When you are hiring cross-generationally to get some young people with fresh skills, you also get an unfamiliar subset of employee requirements. Use your personnel department to traverse the mine field of hiring a twentysomething.

Sales evolvement has been ongoing as well. Twenty years ago the pitch might well have been, "This is a moment in history. You have an opportunity to make a meaningful difference in the success of your organization. Widget manufacturing has been turned upside down by the development of our Widget-producing machine. We are only going to partner with one player in the Widget business in the next two years, and we would like it to be you, but we need to decide today." If you haven't figured it out by now, *this is a joke*. There are people who could still sell this with a straight face, but I would not want them working for me.

In the last fifty years, the corporate landscape has changed dramatically. In the sixties and seventies, the fashion of the day was conglomerates. They were a variety of unrelated portfolio businesses that shared very little with each other. They had their own pension plans, health benefits, and business plans. It was a fleet with no formation; it had no corporate focus, no universal oversight. The stronger chief financial officers were, typically, working for and loyal to the acquired businesses, not in the corporate entity. Usually the parent bought all or most of the insiders' equity holdings. Management was held in place by equity participation in a larger entity over which these managers had virtually no control and, often, in which they had even less interest. Almost all of them failed in the earnings bust of the seventies. In almost every case, the parent company bought a really bad business or two that scuttled the entire enterprise. If the earnings bust did not affect them directly, high interest rates and the lack of available credit finished them off.

From the ashes of the conglomerates, the concept of synergy was born. All of a sudden, synergy was the new yellow brick road to the city of Oz. The easy money of the eighties and nineties became the era of build, buy, and integrate. This was (and still is) the heyday of the multinational mega companies. Look at the current circumstance in the world. Large multinational corporations are liquid and holding more cash than at any time in history. They are flexible and essentially unregulated. They can move labor and production anywhere in the world. They are entities without situs. They have the maximum of flexibility and have used it to their great advantage.

On the flip side, this era also birthed the ideology of "too big to fail." I will not predict what is next in the development of business worldwide, but I will point out that the ability of countries to regulate the practices of and collect taxes from multinational corporations has been meaningfully eroded. For example, Exxon Mobil Corporation, a U.S. corporation and the world's largest integrated oil company, paid fifteen billion in taxes in 2009. Not a penny of that money was paid to the U.S. Treasury. Congress is struggling to control the issuance of derivative securities after the meltdown of 2008. Even if it succeeds, Congress is powerless to control offshore activities, and is challenged to protect the country from another meltdown without passing legislation that would make U.S. financial institutions noncompetitive in the world market.

As a manager, your goal must be to do the best possible job. There are hosts of things you can do to facilitate that outcome. Let us consider a few: Encourage responsible, asymmetrical risk taking. In other words, encourage employees to take risks that have small cost or risk and potentially large payoffs. An example of a good asymmetrical risk was the pet rock: it was low expense—either it works or doesn't—and it has big potential payoff. A bad example would be launching a private-label orange juice company: it is a low-margin business; there are large, entrenched players; and there are high costs of entry. Recognize that most ventures fail. You are measured by successes; being associated with a larger number of smaller risk activities rather than a "career bet" project that doesn't work better serves your career. "Career bet" activities are better executed in a venture capital environment where failure is the norm. Small wins interspaced with inevitable but low-cost failures are expected and essential to excelling as a manager.

However, as a manager you still must think and act like a venture capitalist and a CEO. Ask yourself the following questions: What will it cost? What are our risks if we do this? And perhaps most importantly, what are our risks if we do not do this? What is the expected payoff for the activity? Push this approach down into your organization. Everybody involved must think like an entrepreneur. Employees should frame their thinking by answering the questions above. In the competitive twenty-first century, American business will be driven by the continuous improvement of every aspect of its activities. Do not assume that this does not apply to you; it applies *to everything your organization does.* You leverage yourself by motivating your employees to approach the business the way you approach the business. Different personalities will respond differently. The roosters will have to be beaten back with a stick because they will have ten ideas and you will have to find the good one; the mules will explain why each is impossible or a really bad idea; the scorpion will explain why it is bad for him and should, therefore, be dismissed; and the turtles will do the work to flesh out the plan if you give them sufficient direction. The RITR will lay out her rocks. Once you help her move them, she will get the turtle moving. Your job is to put up with this cacophony of noise and remain focused on finding the good ideas, to advance your career, and to build a demonstrable, scalable management style.

If you have taken and created the management environment I have outlined, you may feel as though you are managing in a chaotic environment. I like to think of it as dynamic, but no matter how you describe it, it is messy. This is a requirement. This is why management pays so well. If you are the kind of person who likes a clear desk and an empty to-do list at the end of the day, this job will make you uncomfortable, at least at the beginning. I have heard management described as lining up the ducks in the pond. The beginning of a new management assignment generates the following image in my mind. You are rowing your boat as fast as you can, grabbing ducks and putting them in a straight line. By the time you get the first few ducks in line, you look back and see the ducks at the beginning of the line have swum off randomly. Management is continuously evolving. Change is the steady state. Fortunately, it does get easier over time. Even ducks can be trained.

There is an old saying in business: "Success has many parents, and failure is an orphan." Share the credit. Nothing erodes your credibility more quickly than being viewed as someone who takes credit for successful ideas and blames others for the failures. That is a simple statement, but I cannot overemphasize how common it is for this insecure behavior on a manager's part to damage the morale of the team. The credit needs to go to the idea person and the implementation team in a visible way. Go out of your way to make sure that credit is public and visible. Your credit is implied; it is your team. Take the bulk of the blame when things go wrong; that's how you build team loyalty. You will fool no one by blaming your team. Your managers will think you are a weasel (no parable required), your peers will use it against you to demonstrate your deficient management skills, and your team will not trust you because you withdrew their air cover at a critical moment in their careers. You will demotivate your team; they will lose confidence in you as a manager. In summary, there is no faster way to unravel the corporate culture you have built than by being a weasel when the mud hits the fan. It may seem like a good idea to blame others when things get really bad, but rest assured, you will fool no one at any level, and the behavior will hound you for the rest of your short career with that organization. (A weasel is always a weasel).

We have now shaped a team and a mission. Positions can be restructured to elicit more turtle and rooster behavior and less mule and scorpion responses. Hire someone who expects things to go wrong and is excited about fixing them when they do. Hire people with the best brains and skills you can find for the money you have to spend. If your employees are smart and skilled, you may feel threatened; get over it and hire them anyway. Corporate life is a foot race. All you can do is run as fast as you can. Don't bother looking over your shoulder. It just increases the wind resistance and slows you down.

Seriously, if you are in this game to win (if you're just in it to break even or lose slowly, you can stop reading now), it is scary but desirable and essential to hire people who are smarter than you and better at doing their jobs than you would be. A year from now, when you are pitching for your well-deserved promotion, the first question you will get is, "Is your replacement ready, willing, and able to step up?" The answer should be yes. If you play it safe and hire a bunch of safe also-rans, you will then be the half-wit leading a team of dopes. In my experience, you will get passed over and backwatered—not promoted. A second-rate team, by definition, has a second-rate manager.

Please remember that you are not hiring bowling buddies. Your employees do not need to be your race, gender, or age. In fact, the less like you they are, the more they potentially bring to the job. It is highly desirable that their first business language is different from your first business language. What do I mean by *business language*? We touched on this earlier, but it is an important concept and worth elaboration. Present a problem to an engineer, and he will try to reengineer the product, service, or process (PSP). Present the same problem to the head of marketing, and she will explain that the PSP is improperly positioned in the marketplace and needs to be properly promoted once it has been repositioned. The sales team will tell you that incentives are required and to run a sales contest. The CFO will explain that the PSP needs to be more profitable to the firm or else it will cannibalize existing PSP business. The lawyers will tell you the PSP is not in compliance with some new law and that it is a business risk to continue offering the PSP at all.

Large firms perform at less than optimal levels, even though they have promoted their best people. Each of those individuals brings his or her first language bias to a new job. Too often new managers speak the same language as the rest of the group they have been promoted to manage. The current view in American business is that moving people between disciplines is too disruptive and too large a hit to productivity. The groupthink is that it takes too long to come up the learning curve. This, of course, like many widely held corporate beliefs, is rubbish.

If those in leadership succumb to employee pressures, they are not leading; they are taking their cues from their hidebound, change-resistant employees. The sales teams will never work for someone who has not "been in the trenches." The marketing team cannot work for someone who is not "a creative." How could the CFO not be an accountant? You want her to run research, and she is not even an engineer? Employees who only want to work with their own kind complain and whine, on and on, until management surrenders. This is so pervasive that if you review the career tracks of CEOs and COOs in large corporations, you will often be able to predict the preferences they bring to the operation of their businesses. They have worked in a silo their entire career. They have the strategic skills and vision of a prairie dog. There are notable exceptions; many great leaders have become multilingual. For the rest of us mortals, we can learn new ways of communicating by getting hands-on experience in various disciplines, a more reliable strategy for developing the flexibility and insight that is required in twenty-first-century corporate America.

Change in corporate practice is a microcosm of change in our society. As the rate of change has accelerated, a new chasm is developing between generations of employees. In *The Singularity Is Near*, Ray Kurzweil focuses on the acceleration of the "rate" of change in almost everything. This acceleration in the speed of change presents extraordinary management challenges. The accelerating speed of the change is becoming a topic for management study and is finding its way into MBA curriculums.

Having recently worked with a charity, I can give an example of the speed of change and its effect on the organization. This young charity had always raised its support money by a combination of personal bequests and gifts from a few targeted foundations. Attracted by the multiyear grants that endowments could offer, the organization was evolving by approaching more endowments and foundations in an effort to expand its fundraising. The board of directors (all middle-aged and older) learned that building these relationships was a multiyear process that would create a funding gap in the early years. To fill that gap, the charity attracted a twenty-six-year-old social media expert who believed that she could use her expertise to open a new channel of contributors, as well as attract a new crop of volunteers, who could also be helpful to the organization.

The previous website of the charity was simple, straightforward, and targeted at an institutional market and the over-forty crowd. It viewed the target as a fifty-five-year-old endowment executive or wealthy contributor. The website designed by the social media expert was culture shock. The expert was sure that her plan was the way to go. Our experienced, fortysomething-year-old fund raiser thought we were nuts. She was sure that any serious contributor or foundation would be turned off by the complexity of the site and the message presented, not to mention the whimsical colors and rotating pictures. The gulf has become so large, even between consecutive generations, that incorporating new ideas has become very threatening to the Baby Boomers' paradigms. This generational gap can generate horizontal silos in which people segregate and associate by generational status and age, in addition to traditional vertical silos that are sorted by functionality.

The complexity of this issue presents a significant management challenge. It places you as a manager in a position to impede or enhance the existing corporate culture. Under normal circumstances, the level of tolerance for silos is an unwritten guideline from the very top of an organization. I am generally a believer in independent decision-making, but I would treat this as an exception to the general rule. Even if there is no formal guidance, your organization has demonstrated many times over its silo tolerance levels.

MANAGING UP

We have spent the bulk of this chapter focusing on managing down, because that is where you need to spend the bulk of your time. Nevertheless, charity begins at home. You do have to deal with your superiors as well. The interactions with your superiors are just as important to your future as a successful manager as your interactions with those who report to you. When you change jobs internally or externally, you often have an opportunity to influence the decision as to who your new boss should be. If you are changing firms, you get a chance to interview your prospective boss in advance. That meeting supplies you with important information on whether or not to accept a new position. In fact, it may be your single most important input. It is easy to think of the power as in the hands of the hiring manager. I urge you to exercise your power as a decision-maker. You are much more likely to be offered a job that you interviewed the employer for than in the more traditional fashion of him interviewing you.

Your new boss does not have to be your best friend, but it helps. You will find at this point that my approach may seem contradictory (which at least shows you were paying attention); that's because it is contradictory. Throughout this book, I have avoided the subjects of fair and random bad luck. To achieve a better than average outcome in a competitive environment, you must work hard to stack the deck in your favor. We have spent a lot of time on why humans act the way they act and how to predict what they will do in a given situation. You would love to have a different relationship with your boss than your employees have with you. So do not recommend this book to him or her. If your boss wants to be your friend and socialize outside of work, if he or she genuinely seems to like you and wants to deepen the personal relationship, go for it. On balance it is likely good for your future.

It is a bad idea for you to hire employees like yourself, but it is an excellent idea for you to work for someone like yourself. That person is more likely to appreciate your approach and to be a mentor to you. Simply put, you are more likely to be the beneficiary of positive bias, which is good for your career. It is not a great idea to create bias when you are the boss. As an employee, a little down-home bias is great for performance reviews. Let us be crystal clear here: I am talking about social relationships, not sexual relationships. *Keep your pants or skirt on at work*. No good *ever* comes out of something as emotionally charged as a romantic relationship between boss and subordinate.

Another approach, which applies more to internal transfers or changing firms to join a former superior at their new firm, and virtually always works, is to select a boss who has "saved your cookies"—bailed you out of a jam or gone out on a limb to advance your career in the past. There is no logical reason why someone who has helped you once should develop a greater sense of responsibility and become more invested in advancing your career. Let me assure you, logic notwithstanding, the behavior is commonplace and predictable. In psychology there is a theory of cognitive dissonance; this is the reverse application of that concept.

People are not comfortable with logical inconsistencies. If a person helps someone once, she has made a bet on that person's talent level. She will help you repeatedly because it validates her original judgment. I like the idea of a boss who is predisposed to help my career for any reason. It would be nice if I deserved support, but even if it is only to reinforce his or her original actions and conclusions, I'll will take it anyway. Work is not school; there will be winners and losers. Sometimes the venture is so successful that everyone wins, but the real winners win bigger. I would never suggest engaging in any behavior that causes you to be uncomfortable with the ethics or morality of the activity. As counterpoint, you must be alert to every advantage that may be presented to you.

A new boss represents a high-risk, unpredictable moment in your career—no matter how good you are at your job. Think long and hard when you consider career changes that involve leaving a good boss who gives you great "air cover" (watches out for you and backs up your decisions). Do not underestimate the importance of a "new boss risk premium," which is translated as a lot more money or a sharply tilted career track. You are not a wimp for staying with a good boss and turning down a small increase and so-so promotion across the street.

A more general risk occurs when mergers take place. You are much more likely to lose your job if you get a boss from the other side of a business combination. There is no cognitive dissonance to protect your job. New bosses tend to get rid of people to whom they have no personal loyalty.

Do everything you can to avoid this outcome. At this junction, you need to be the squeaky wheel: you must communicate, directly, that you know what is expected of a good employee. (Look down a few paragraphs to build a script.) This is the time, when the fog of change is thick, to tack away from your counterparts and chart your own course. In this situation, when there is blood in the water, "if you run with sheep, you will end up a lamb chop." Be loud and clear. You must do everything you can for your reports, but your counterparts are on their own. Team loyalty in a crisis is vertical first (to your current directs); horizontal loyalty and solidarity is a luxury item.

My experience with bosses joining from other firms and departments is that they tend to create an environment that is less conducive to the creation of silos, but they also create higher turnover and do more damage to morale. There is no resolution to this dilemma. Many companies operate on the view that "it is the dead wood that holds up the tree." Others want to run lean and mean with no silos. The first are too concerned about morale and family values. The other extreme is to undervalue their importance. Unless you are running the company, you will not be able to influence which policy is embedded in the bones of the organization.

To survive and flourish in either environment, you must quickly determine which environment you are in: dead wood or slash and burn. Forget what management or, even worse, human resources say; watch their behavior and be prepared to adjust your thinking on the fly.

Let us talk about what it takes to be a good employee, to be the rooster, but let's leave the barnyard behind for the moment for the sake of clarity. It takes everything we have demanded from our direct reports as outlined in this chapter. Now we need to communicate it effectively. We must communicate the following: I am aligned—I am on mission. I know what I need to do. I take full responsibility, and I will see to it that it gets done (the rooster). I am loyal—I recognize that my path to success is to make you look good.

If you can communicate these two simple messages to your superiors, you have gone a long way toward building a relationship with your new boss. She becomes comfortable that you are not trying to undermine her, making her feel safe and letting her know that you have it. You have verbalized that you can and will do the job she needs done. This is a stressful time; everyone wants to feel safe before welcoming a new team member.

MANAGING ACROSS

Managing across is the soft underbelly of management practice. Dealing with your counterparts is always a challenge. These folks, at the most fundamental level, are your competition. They compete with you in different ways depending on the structure and practices of your organization. They may be a threat to your job, the scope of your responsibilities, or the resources available to pay you the bonus you want. They may be after your best people or in competition with you for your boss's job. In a typical silo environment, the individual cultures of each silo are radically different.

They are fashioned by the personal style of their leaders. In truth, these counterparts can be difficult to deal with. Often one or two of them flat out do not like you, and you do not feel any more warmly about them. Even the ones you do like and respect may take a shot at you if you turn your back or show weakness in the form of a few bad calls.

Some of them are intimidating; they make you wonder if they are doing better with the boss than you are. Others are dumb and random; you wonder why they even have their jobs and probably speculate that your personal organization and power base would be so much better if some or all of their areas reported to you. This is very likely the greatest source of wasted time in corporate America. An extraordinary amount of time, energy, creativity, and emotional venting are directed at getting even, winning, looking better, or hurting the competition.

The boss hates this (although he likely engages in the same activity at his level). He views it as you wasting your time. You bring him questions and decisions that he thinks should be settled at your level with your counterparts. You are also running through a minefield, barefoot and blindfolded. As we discussed earlier, there are secret connections all around. Every time you point out someone else's weakness, you are rubbing your manager's nose in a mess he is likely already aware of. There may well be special circumstances or connections that you are not privy to (e.g., he is not going to fire his girlfriend's sister, even though he understands that she is not much of a contributor).

Stay wrapped in the corporate flag. Align yourself with the mission and never argue that something is better for you, personally. Argue that it is in the corporate interest to do it your way. Seize the moral high ground and hold on to it for dear life. That may sound silly, but everything you do will be highly visible. You cannot fight based on your gut. You must develop your rationale as to why giving you more power, control, or scope of responsibilities is in the corporation's best interest. Stay with your themes. Seek to improve them, but don't be afraid to repeat your themes over and over again. This is a ground war. It is won inch by inch. Never fight a battle you cannot win. Focus on the ones you can win. You must, of course, earn to tell the difference. Accept the idea that as you push for more power or scope, you may have to give up other things. This is like a card game; you are trying to upgrade your hand, but you can only do it by discarding cards you do not need.

Kill your colleagues with kindness. Lower the silo wall and invite them onto your decision-making committees, as long as there is a quid pro quo. Extol the virtue of open communication and lead by example. Build alliances—the more comprehensive the better. Information is power; if you are in the loop, you are being empowered. If you are doing it by the book, you have built your culture and your team. Now you can devote more time and energy to your "across the aisle" activities.

This is not about the personalities. Remember you are tightly wrapped in the corporate flag. You are standing on the moral high ground and wearing your white hat. Save the vendettas: they are considered unprofessional and coun-terproductive. Do not dig in on the idea of one solution. Do not "call the question" unless you are sure you have the votes. If you lay a report on the boss's desk seeking a radical change, it is ninety-ten against you. Any contested change is no better than a fifty-fifty bet under the best of circum-stances. Never forget that your boss hates the intramurals. He always wants you to reach a settlement and bring it to him so that he can simply say, "Great job. Now go do it."

Most of these battles are normal corporate stuff. Marketing and sales are always at each other's throats. There is never a clear picture of why something fails or succeeds. Client service thinks that product development exists to torture them. Product development works with sales over what can be sold but never with client service as to what can be supported. You cannot go to war over the normal stresses of business. You must be prepared to deal and fight, if necessary, only about the abnormal stresses, the ones that threaten your corporate well-being or actually represent a risk to the enterprise.

Going for the kill shot is one of business's greatest temptations. Everyone occasionally finds himself in posi-tion of knowing enough bad stuff about an internal com-petitor to try and get him fired. In chess, there is an open-ing that involves being offered the "poison pawn" (the queen's knights pawn). If you are playing an able competi-tor, you will usually be sorry if you take the pawn. It looks like a safe move, but the game just turns against you from that point. Going for the kill shot is a lot like taking the poison pawn. It may work, but the odds are against you. If you go to your boss to complain about a counterpart, you are probably making a mistake. Your boss does not want to hear it; it is a distraction. No matter how you put it, it will not be viewed as in pursuit of a corporate benefit; it will be viewed as a personal attack. It will likely fail to accomplish anything. More often than not, it will result in no change.

We spoke previously about secrets. Based on that discussion, I can virtually assure you that the person you are attacking will find out about the allegation. Now you have an active enemy who will feel justified in launching a shooting war. He has the moral high ground, because you started it. The rest of the organization will view the whole thing as an amusing but unproductive catfight. You will be famous, but not in a good way. These silly battles often end in a double drowning: you are so busy fighting with each other you end up drowned at the bottom of the corporate pool with your arms wrapped around each other. While you engage in a battle you likely cannot win, your other competitors will advance their careers at your expense.

Look for a smarter solution. Take the advice of the great Chinese general Sun Tzu (*The Art of War*): only fight battles you are certain you can win. It was true in the sixth century and it is equally true today. For many managers, situations like this become an important measure of their ability to engage in adult behavior. Management pays well in part because you must suffer the ongoing frustration of subtle gains or losses. Rarely do you get a clean win; often you do not even know the outcome of the skirmish.

If all else fails and you must take this shot (which I urge you not to do), be deadly. *Shoot to kill.* I mean dead, indicted, fired on the spot, and escorted from the building. Fire ten bullets, not one bullet, including headshots. A wounded competitor is like a pissed-off tiger. If you shoot and don't kill, drop the gun and run. However, even succeeding usually results in career disruption. In my experience, most successful killers end up leaving the company in the following year. Everyone knows what you have done; they also think, rightly or wrongly, that you are out for blood. They are afraid of you, and they don't trust you. You will be cut off from information; your ability to do your job or advance your career will be impaired. Even when you move on to your next firm, your reputation may follow you.

SUMMARY

1. The past predicts the future, but with imperfect timing.
2. All businesses think they are unique and yet they are all very similar.
3. Create a corporate culture.
4. Secrets are for dead people.
5. When dealing with your reports, avoid personal relationships.
6. Encourage decision-making in uncertainty. It is OK to make errors if the analyses are conducted properly.
7. Reward courage. You need people who are not afraid to tell you, privately, that you are wrong.
8. Stress that first-mover advantage (being first to market) is more important than certainty.

9. Take the blame, give the credit.
10. Execution and accountability are everything.
11. Get rid of or minimize the people who cannot adapt to the new culture.
12. Integrate sales into the business development function.
13. Don't fight the Silo wars.
14. Build alliances that open the information flow as long as it flows both ways.
15. Stay company-focused: remember the name on the paycheck, and do not be afraid to remind your reports.
16. When you deal with your counterparts, stay on the high ground. Do not fire the first shot, no matter how tempted you are.
17. When you deal with your boss, be sure he knows that you are focused on making him look good.
18. Work on your personal relationship with your manager.

Management requires flexibility and imagination; it requires a long-term plan and goals combined with a clear understanding that the plan for success is never fully or correctly formed when you start and will be in need of constant revision. You must keep your eyes on the goal, which is in the distance, but remember that you cannot afford to break your neck by tripping over the bumps in the road along the way.

CHAPTER 2

Leadership

I f I were describing the primary element of quality leadership, it would be the gift to bear, seemingly effortlessly, the responsibility of developing, embracing, and selling the vision and long-term business plans and principals of your organization. Leadership requires making a few lonely decisions when there are rational and valid views from smart people on both sides of the issue. This happens more than you might think. The stakes associated with these decisions are high. Sometimes the success or failure of the enterprise is determined by the outcome.

Leadership is the ability to communicate every aspect of the vision to each employee with all the information he or she needs to know, in a way and to a level of specificity that he or she can understand. Furthermore, revealing the vision should be accomplished while concealing any trace of uncertainty or insecurity you may have associated with the plan. At the same time, you cannot overstate the potential opportunities or understate the risk of failure.

The reason the person in charge makes the big bucks is that this skill is not trainable. I do not know how you would train to do this. It may be the essence of the commonly held view that leaders are born, not made. Leadership is not something they teach effectively in business school, and other jobs in management are not necessarily preparatory for the task. Many times in my career, I could pass the heavy lifting, the really difficult calls, up the line to the CEO. It was a relief to get those tough decisions off my plate. When I became CEO of an organization, the stress of making the tough calls took an emotional toll.

The following statement was excerpted from an article in the *Wall Street Journal* entitled "Investing in Well-Managed Companies," by Scott Adams, the creator of *Dilbert*. It ran June 5, 2010. Although it is entertaining, it also addresses how ill-defined and ephemeral leadership is as a concept.

INVESTING IN WELL-MANAGED COMPANIES

When companies make money, we assume they are well-managed. That perception is reinforced by the CEOs of those companies who are happy to tell you all the clever things they did to make it happen. The problem with relying on this source of information is that CEOs are highly skilled in a special form of lying called leadership. Leadership involves convincing employees and investors that the CEO has something called a vision, a type of optimistic hallucination that can come true only in an environment in which the CEO is massively overcompensated and the employees have learned to be less selfish.

Scott is more willing than I am to share value judgments about leaders. On the other hand, he can be pretty funny, so I'll cut him some slack. The leader in battle—and you are always in battle—must wear a red shirt. (In medieval times, the king would wear a red shirt into battle so that if he were injured, the troops would not see blood and lose courage.) There is nowhere for you to share your insecurities. As CEO, you are the steward of the vision and the plan; you live in a glass bowl. Expect that everything you do or say will be viewed under intense magnification. People in power are always deified or vilified (typically, one and then the other).

Those I coach always ask, "What is the real secret of effective leadership?" There is no simple answer to that question. My experience suggests that four behaviors are required to be an effective leader.

1. Remain open-minded and accepting of out-of-the-box creative thinking.
2. Be personally and passionately invested in the outcomes.
3. Use emotional appeals to inspire, direct, and motivate.
4. Be actively, visibly, and confidently engaged in deci-sion-making in the face of ambiguity.

As you rise through the ranks, you become responsible for greater numbers of people and a greater number of decisions. You become less connected to each person and decision. Your role has shifted. You must now be a visionary and work hard to get the most out of the people charged with executing. You need to focus on long-term outcomes. "Is the organization moving in the right direction?" is the question that should keep you up at night.

Buddha spent his whole life saying he was just a man like any other. During my travels in Sri Lanka, I saw many people in Buddhist temples burning incense and praying for good luck or guidance. Buddha was deified—despite his advice to the contrary. It is a little strange that everything else he said was accepted as what has now become the equivalent of gospel by more than one billion people. Irrespective of his brilliant insights, Buddha missed a critical understanding of human behavior. In the end, it is not what you say that matters, only the part of what you say that is embraced by the listener. Followers were enraptured by Buddha's message. They wanted and needed his proclamations to be true. It was easier for them to make that leap if he was a god, not just the smart and thoughtful man he claimed to be.

You are the boss. Everyone around you is reading your facial expressions and your body language. If you had a fight with your spouse, everyone will be thinking about the implications of your bad mood. Your comments are being interpreted at a micro level. People will often see or hear things that you are not trying to communicate...or trying not to communicate. Sometimes they are focusing on nothing, but just as often they are sensing an uncertainty of which you may not be consciously aware. If this sounds like a lonely job, you are very perceptive. You may be too insecure to wear the leadership mantle. If that is the case, get a shrink or a mentor. Another approach might be to recognize your own strengths and weaknesses; maybe a better choice for you would be to stay in senior management, turn down the promotion to lonely leadership, and get a dog. Having sat in that leader seat for many years, I can assure you that the isolation is intense and the inability to express actual reactions and emotions is exhausting. Not everyone is cut out for it, and honest reflection should temper your desire to win the brass ring or get to the top. It can be added that if something really goes bad in the business, it is always your fault and you will very likely take the fall for the outcomes. The Apple board fired Steve Jobs for early mistakes at that firm. We know how that worked out.

Leadership techniques and skills are easy to talk about but difficult to identify and practice. Some argue that leadership skills are inborn and cannot be learned. Either you have them, or you are out of luck. I do not fully believe that, or this book would be a chapter shorter. Life is certainly easy if you are born knowing how to be a leader. In the early nineties, I had the fortune—or misfortune, depending on whom you ask—of working briefly for Jamie Dimon (CEO of J.P. Morgan). He was the president and rising star at Smith Barney Shearson. Under Jamie's leadership, that firm went on to merge with Citibank and become the largest and most successful bank on earth. As a side note, all of the bad things that happened at Citibank took place long after Dimon left and took the important talent with him. Simply stated, he was the best, smartest, and most insightful manager I had ever worked for, but he was not inspirational and could not excite me (or most other people) about the big picture. At that time, I thought he was only a fair leader. It appears from his performance at J.P. Morgan that time has allowed him to develop the skills and maturity to become the fine leader and great manager he is today. It has been said that leadership is like pornography; you may not be able to define it exactly, but you know it when you see it.

There are two challenges to being an effective leader: You have to keep a straight face while expressing a level of optimism that you may not actually feel (e.g., "We have the best employees in the world," or "We have the strongest product line," or "We have the best plan," or "We understand the market, and we are emphasizing the right areas."). You also need to use superlatives that feel forced under normal circumstances (e.g., *best, strongest,* etc.). You must radiate certainty and confidence, even though you may be neither certain nor fully confident. These are not normal circumstances. Being a leader or CEO is not a normal job.

When good employees become unduly worried about the future of the company, they do one of two things: they freeze like deer in the headlights, or worse, they start edging toward the door so they can find another job before the company fails. Either way, they compromise your enterprise. It is a lot like being a religious leader in a house of worship. People expect you to assure them about things of which you have incomplete empirical evidence. What you do have is a clearer vision of the future than they have, and they are comforted by that vision and your confidence in it.

If you are a normal person and not a megalomaniac, adopting the behavior described above and always appearing fully confident may make you feel uncomfortable. Worse yet, you may feel exposed or even silly and contrived. You assume everyone can see through this blatant ruse and is laughing at you. You are suffering from inside-outside syndrome. You assume that because you feel disingenuous on the inside, you appear disingenuous to your constituency. Nothing could be further from the truth. Your employees want to believe your vision. People worship sports teams, join social clubs, and go to church on Sunday or temple or mosque on Saturdays. They want to feel part of something, and they want to adopt the values of their fellow members. That is why, at company meetings, they hang onto the leader's every word and try to interpret every inflection.

Perhaps more importantly, if you feel uncomfortable, you are comparing your insides to other people's outsides. You are not transparent. People see only what you show them, not your secret fears and insecurities. This is a difficult concept. No one wants to write a book entitled *Just Lie to Them*. It is difficult to remain focused, optimistic, and committed to your vision without making irresponsible statements. That balance is an essential element of leadership. Great leaders seem to find a way to do it effortlessly while appearing earnest in their beliefs.

Virtually everyone is shy about some area of communication. A famous public speaking coach suggests that if you are uncomfortable speaking in front of a large group, you should visualize your audience naked. The theory is, if they are exposed, you will feel less exposed. I would rather that you visualize yourself perfectly dressed. People always *appear* more confident in their interactions than you *feel* about your interactions. (People also look better dressed than they do naked) This is a normal reaction. Most of us who are driven to great success are driven, at least in part, by our insecurities. In my view, the need to win is always tied to the personal implications and fears of losing.

Leadership is an intense exercise in public speaking. If you are speaking to the press or to your board of directors, you are making public statements for which you will be held responsible. The good news is that nobody can read your mind. You must accept that your statements will be accepted largely at face value. That will not discourage folks from speculating about what you left out or really meant to say. Almost everyone is a wreck on the inside compared to what they portray publicly. It is a leap of faith to believe that no one really sees your mushy inside. Let me assure you, I have never given a speech without being nervous, but my mushy inside has always remained invisible. I have also watched many people I have coached address their organizations. I knew they were wrecks inside, but I could not detect their discomfort by watching them speak. This public role is not for everyone, but there is no way to become a leader without crossing the divide. Remember, you must guard against comparing your insides with other people's outsides.

When you communicate as a leader, impart knowledge. Information is optional. Your management structure is based on supplying information. Your managers are well equipped to deliver information. You must focus on all forms of collecting information. My first experience with leadership came almost fifty years ago. My brother-in-law, Albert Gewirtz, owned and operated a hot dog, donut, pizza, and knish shop on the boardwalk in Long Beach, Long Island. Every summer morning, Albee would go out and walk the boards—two long blocks, in both directions—to get the rhythm of the day. Was the surf up? Was the wind blowing onshore or offshore? Was there a haze that will keep the heat down? Was the crowd old or young? With this information, he could call the day: how many people in help did he need to work that day, how many donuts and knishes to bake, and what to feature at the front of the store. He could not quantify what he had learned, but it helped him formulate his bet for that day. He started every day by collecting information. He was a great leader; I often went on these walks with him, and I was convinced that the information he collected on these walks actually made him a better decision-maker and donut-baker.

Structure your day to create some walking around time, either physically or by telephone. Walking around allows informal, unstructured interactions across many levels of management to take place. The telephone is a good aid when actual walking around is not feasible. This is a leadership activity. Management, by its nature, is more process driven. E-mailing, despite its ease of use and the reduced emotional toll on you, is not a good substitute. It is too impersonal, and it exists forever. You are aware of this and so is any smart employee. That constraint prevents it from having the desired result of allowing you to collect useful, informal, or off-the-record information. Anyone who has ever worked for a company that has been sued knows that, when things go wrong, every e-mail is read and interpreted in the worst possible context. Speaking in person or on the telephone is your chance to get unfiltered feedback about the pulse of the place. If your direct reports have read the management chapter of this book, they are protecting you from the unpleasant details or anything that makes them look bad.

The walk around is one of the only organized, systematic ways for a leader to collect unfiltered, back-channel information. This is your chance to listen, to engage in informal conversation. Do not argue, do not take notes, and do not try to fix anything on the fly. This is your rare opportunity to come across as human and interactive. Talk about sports, golf, food, family, or about the business or business environment. Control your desire to speak. Be interested in what your employees have to say, collect the information, and let it help you feel the rhythm of the company. Remember how you felt when you started: if someone in a position of power stopped at your desk just to shoot the breeze, it was a big deal to you.

Subjective input should come to you from an unfiltered source; your direct reports cannot be depended upon to give you the real tone of the place. Protect your informal sources. Help the employees feel safe in these interactions, but stop short of saying something formal and constraining like "off the record." It is important for you to keep your credibility. If you work for all the stakeholders of your organization, "off the record" is not a promise you can keep with certainty.

Your direct reports will give you the facts and figures to the level of detail you require. At the same time, they are your management responsibility. They need to be managed as well as led. They cannot be managed by walking around. Do not fall into the trap of abandoning your formal management process simply because you passed their desks while on patrol. They still require a structured, organized, and formal approach to their career development. Just because you have become a leader does not mean you can stop being an effective manager.

Treat everyone with respect. Demand that you be treated that way and demand that employees treat each other that way. Be prepared to make an example of someone. You are not only the CEO, you are also the chief culture officer. You set the rules, and you make them nonnegotiable. Every employee needs to hear the rules from you, directly or indirectly. Be sure the tone is such that everyone understands that you are deadly serious and not just paying lip service by reading the compliance officer's boilerplate. The culture of your organization actually does start with you. You can put your own stamp on how people treat each other and, therefore, how the entity behaves.

Sam Walton knew that his employees were the path to the continuous improvement of product and process. He went to great lengths to get into the trenches and ask his employees how to serve customers better. He knew that the frontline employees, the ones who touch the customers, knew how to create a more positive shopping experience. He was driven to collect and utilize those insights. When you look at Wal-Mart today, you have to wonder if some of that zeal to improve died with Sam Walton. In many ways, his behavior typifies what a great leader should be. He kept an open mind and an honest willingness to reinvent the organization, iteratively, based on what he had learned. He also demonstrated the courage to abandon things that worked well in order to implement things that worked even better.

Use the ugly side of human behavior for good. If you are old enough, you remember the chilling book and movie *Lord of the Flies*, in which a group of boys, left on their own on an uninhabited island, devolve into savages. They develop a groupthink that rationalizes the most extreme behavior. Another example of this is the lynch mob that feels perfectly justified. Everyone is of the same mind. In old Westerns, a brave sheriff stands up to the mob and makes an impassioned speech for legal process, and often turns the tide. He provides adult supervision and is able to break the groupthink trance. Sometimes that doesn't work, and the mob hangs him too.

Attend a college football game at a Big Ten school, and you will see crazy behavior. The fans' over the top behavior is reinforced by other crazy fans. There is no voice of reason in the crowd. Anyone rooting for the visiting team keeps his or her mouth shut for fear of being beaten up. Murders have taken place between fans of rival soccer teams at games around the world. This stuff is high-octane; it represents a leadership opportunity. Groupthink has associated risks that need to be managed.

If you have attended a political convention or any emotionally charged event, you have felt the electricity of like-minded people reinforcing each other's enthusiasm and conviction. Just watching a national political convention on TV causes a bump in the polls. Some people are induced to join the party just by observing the party's unbridled spirit. As much as we may consider ourselves independent thinkers, most of us are meaningfully influenced by the effects of groupthink. We will cover this in greater detail in the next chapter.

Group omnipotence is scary. Yet it is a powerful leadership tool. For better or worse, people want to believe! People seek a way to be part of something larger than themselves. They derive a sense of well-being from joining something that helps them feel safe or powerful. If that something is exclusive, they feel even more empowered. Good examples might be a fraternity or sorority, an adult fraternal organization, or a country club. Members are surrounded by people who share their values. The opinion of the general populace is suddenly less visible and less important. It often creates a mechanism to shut out the perceived inconsistency and shortcomings of our society. Life feels a little safer. Their path seems clearer. Their views are being reinforced, and all is good with the world. This should sound like a good corporate culture model.

As the leader, your goal is to figure out a way to successfully harness all this good stuff. As I have said, people want to believe. If you believe in what you say, they will believe in you. For some of you that may be a terrifying thought. Of course, it is terrifying. This is the challenge that comes with leadership. This is why leaders die young and get paid more. You are the final decision-maker. When you make a decision, you will be held accountable for the outcome. If you delay too long, you will be viewed as weak and indecisive. If you move too quickly, you will be labeled a loose cannon. You must get the timing right, and you have to believe it and sell it with complete conviction.

George Bush landed on an aircraft carrier and said, "Mission accomplished." Even though he was later vilified—justifiably, because he was wrong by a mile—at the time he was an inspirational leader. Barack Obama left the Gulf oil spill remediation to British Petroleum (BP) for the first forty-five days. Even though everyone agreed it was BP's responsibility and that BP was certainly more qualified than the U.S. government to accomplish the cleanup, Obama was universally viewed as not providing great leadership. The CEO of British Petroleum acted fine by normal standards. Yet as a leader, he has been an embarrassment. He had the nerve to say, "I want my life back," and had the nerve to respond forthrightly to call the congressional representatives "clowns" when they grandstanded at his expense. When Barack Obama killed Osama bin Laden in a daring raid with high-tech helicopters and Navy SEALs, he was a strong leader. If the raid had failed, he would have been Jimmy Carter and on his way to political oblivion.

The standard for communication is high. As a leader, you are an actor. You will be judged not only by what you say but also by how and when you say it. Your employees are keeping score as to how convincingly you deliver the message and how sincere you appear while doing it. Buddha reminds us, it's what the people hear, not what you say. That is why verbal communication is so challenging.

In the seventies, I was in management at an old-line brokerage firm called E.F. Hutton & Co. At that time, our leader was a gentleman named George Ball, who had achieved his position by a meteoric rise through the ranks at the firm. I attended a sales meeting at which George was trying to motivate my counterparts and me so that we could, in turn, rally the troops to keep fighting in the face of a horrible business environment. The situation was bleak; the bear market had started in 1969 and persisted into the late seventies. There were brief rallies, but nothing worked for long. George stood, smiled, and said the following: "This situation creates an extraordinary opportunity for us. E.F. Hutton is uniquely positioned to take advantage of the situation and capture an improved position in our industry. Destiny is on our side." He smiled, laid out the plan in good detail, and told us he believed that, with this plan and our commitment, "Success is inevitable." The plan involved getting from where we were to the other side of the mountain. George explained, "We are going to walk around the mountain. If that doesn't work, we'll climb over the mountain. If our path is blocked, we will tunnel under the mountain. If all else fails, we'll move the whole damn mountain." He believed it. I believed it, and I was going out to buy shovels.

So what is a safe inspirational speech? There isn't one. In the end, you must commit to your vision. You must imply that you have better information; you must imply that, by virtue of being the leader, you have better judgment; you must communicate your unqualified belief in the plan. On the other hand, the responsibility for execution must clearly be laid at the feet of all the employees. You sketch the vision. They bring the paint.

Your goal is to create common purpose; to sketch your vision of the firm's goals and end products or outcomes: "Our goal is to reshape the world into a better place. Everything we commit to is focused on that purpose." "We will produce the world's greatest widget. With extraordinary execution, we will have an ROI of 20 percent and the special, state-of-the-art features of our Widgets will result in our domination of the marketplace. We will hire the best and brightest, we will crush the competition, we will be a great corporate citizen, and we will reward our stakeholders for their vision and hard work."

Do not immerse yourself in the details. If you can cost-effectively add value by digging into small decisions, you have the wrong people working on the team or you are in the wrong job. Stay focused: Why are we doing this? What will it cost? What will it do? When will it be ready? Delegate everything you can, except leadership itself.

Cynicism and cronyism are gone. You no longer have the luxury of flip remarks or a posse to take to lunch. Go to lunch with your direct reports and fulfill your management responsibilities, or go with employee groups to answer their vision and opportunity questions. You are being watched like a hawk watches a mouse. Force yourself to wave the flag and be optimistic even when it feels disingenuous. Focus on what the future will bring, not on which road the company is traveling to get there. Ignore the temptation to supply details. That is their manager's job.

Focus on "Why are we doing this?" and the end product. Take your managers' input and incorporate it when it is relevant to the plan. Utilize their participation to require them to own the vision with you. Communicate to them that they are leaders-in-training and need to sing from the same hymnbook. Demand their loyalty. Clearly explain that their loyalty is not a request but a job requirement! Remember, every senior manager is in training to be a great leader. If you don't think he can do it, you need to ask yourself why he is in senior management.

Management's job begins at this point. The managers need to finish fleshing out this joint vision and creating the answers to the following questions: Who does what? How long will it take? How much will it cost? How much money will we make? You have built the plan and the management team. Now, you must take the leap of faith, *launch the dragon,* turn the aircraft carrier into the wind (required to launch an attack), and empower your managers and motivate them to delegate the responsibilities and execute the plan. "The enemy is before us, victory is within our reach, you are the point of the spear. Execute!"

Leadership

Leadership is the ability to inspire, build consensus, align interests, create vision, and delegate. If this sounds easy, maybe you were born to lead. If management adopts your vision, you can step aside and let your management team do the work. If the managers don't adopt your vision after that speech, rethink your management team.

A separate challenge of leadership is wrestling with the problem of silo drift. As a reminder, a silo is a method of running an activity within the confines of a larger enterprise. For instance, you are in charge of selling your company's consumer products. All of the consumer product salespeople report to you. Over the years, you have hired marketing people to meet your "specialty needs." You have your own IT development team so you can allocate and prioritize your unique development needs more efficiently. You have your own lawyers and accountants as well; after all, your books need to be perfect, and your legal challenges are unique to your business. If you noticed the transition in this paragraph, you started as the manager of an activity and finished as the CEO of a business. That is the creation of a silo.

This is like the struggle between the ocean and the beach. There are brilliant and irrefutable arguments for and against silos. I have heard this discussion a hundred times. In general, the stronger the manager, the more successful she is in building her silo. Managers want to "silo up." It makes them feel more powerful. It also makes them feel safe. Why wouldn't it? Nobody on the outside has any idea what is going on in their silos. The more reports you have, the more important and CEO-like you appear. The more resources you control, the more independent your decision-making process becomes. After all, in management, the one who has the most reports when he or she dies wins. Silos make it easier to claim credit for your wins and ignorance of other's failures. (After all, you cannot be expected to know what is going on in someone else's silo.)

Within a strong silo, normal risk-management influences are dampened. The lawyers and accountants who would normally sound an alarm associated with illegality or imprudent risk-taking are co-opted. The accountants and lawyers are on the silo's payroll; they get paid based on how well their silo does as a business entity, not based on how sharp their legal minds are or how good their accounting skills are. As a result, "siloization" fosters risk-taking. We have recently seen this effect in the Wall Street meltdown. Groups headed by thirty something geniuses from top business schools were running profit centers that were classical silos. They did the math. If you make a leveraged bet with someone else's money and win, you get rich and famous. If you lose, you go to another employer and try it again. The need to foster or control risk-taking must be factored into any policy relating to silos within your organization.

Let's play a game. How many of these have you heard: "I need specialists, not the generalists that the firm supplies." (The firm doesn't know how to hire.) "I need to be able to prioritize the workload." (Everybody who doesn't work for me is lazy, stupid, or both.) "I need to set the cultural norms in my group so people know what is expected of them." (I have to control the flow of information so no one makes us look bad.) "The guy running the institutional product group has his own dedicated resources. If I don't have the same, I am operating at a disadvantage." (I don't feel powerful! He is getting more people than I am. Therefore, he will become more important than I am, and he will win the promotion race.) "I tried it the other way at my last firm. I know it does not work." (My mind is made up, and I will say anything to get extra power.) "Everything that controls my outcomes must report to me." (I am a control freak and power monger. I admit it).

Any organization must communicate with the outside world in a seamless fashion. The message delivered should be the same in tone as in content, no matter how the outsider (client, vender, media, etc.) accesses that information. In the new world of communication (websites, Twitter, the addition of Asian call centers, people working from home, and all the other challenges of complex, multinational organizations operating twenty-four hours a day, seven days a week), these challenges are magnified in an organization that operates in silos. The secretive nature and competitive environment in which silos operate exacerbate an already difficult communication and messaging challenge.

Communication is a vital internal and external challenge for all organizations. Businesses have been destroyed by the corporate warfare that goes on between interested parties who have struggled to control the mentality of the organization. Managers want to operate in silos, in part because it reduces their need to collaborate. It is human nature to elevate your personal skills to a level of importance that trivializes the contributions of others with different skills.

Professional athletes and movie stars epitomize this behavior, but it exists in all human beings. A star salesperson is often dismissive of a good brand or well-constructed product when describing his or her success. In fact, you will often hear tales of success that are framed as "Despite the bad brand or weak product, I prevailed." Some writers have attributed such behavior to greed: "If it is more *me* than *us*, I should be paid more for what I do." I wish it were that simple. In my experience, in every discipline there is an "arrogance of importance" (AOI). The chief financial officer (CFO) always thinks the answers are in the numbers, and every group with a budget thinks the CFO is penny wise and pound foolish. The classic complaint is: the finance guys never see the big picture and don't understand that "you have to spend money to make money." The chief legal officer (CLO) believes the answers are in the law or the rules as regulators have decreed. She doesn't appreciate the concept of taking business risks when the stakes are high. Marketers think salespeople are a bunch of fast-talking idiots who have it easy if the branding and positioning are performed properly. Sales believe marketing is a waste of time and that business would improve if you just raised sales' payouts. Client service is the heart and soul of any business and needs to be involved from beginning to end—just ask the client service people. Without a doubt, what makes or breaks every product launch is a properly researched and designed product. Anyone in new product development will confirm this for you.

Do you have a headache yet? I'm getting one just writing this section. There are many positives to silos. Unfortunately, the benefits do not outweigh the inherent conflicts and risks associated with them. You have three choices at this juncture. First, live with the silos. Plenty of companies do, and many of them seem to do fine. Second, if you want the gold standard, run a one profit and loss (P&L) company. This will create a silo-free environment. You cannot run a silo if you do not have your own P&L. This will create a cultural revolution in your organization. Good employees will leave, so turnover will increase. You will need to revamp your incentive systems and adjust the perspectives of your management team. Everyone will hate it, and many of your employees will hate you for going in this direction. Long-term, your organization may be better off, but short-term momentum will be lost, and you will have to put up with months of people arguing why this will never work. Many small companies start out with this one P&L approach. As they grow, strong managers convince inexperienced leaders that greater specialization and "more robust vertical organizational methodology" (the seeds of silos) are required to foster productivity and accountability. A third choice involves a compromise. Let's call it "silos with training wheels." You create the illusion of an independent operation and still protect the company from truly insane behavior that could jeopardize the entire enterprise. It is like "Lord of the Flies" with hall monitors. The compromise requires a top-to-bottom structural mandate that must be decreed from the top levels of the firm. This involves "vertical corporate stakes" in a "silo" world. All lawyers report to the firm's legal department. All accountants report to the office of the CFO. All marketing personnel have at least a dotted-line report to the marketing department, period; no exceptions. Let sales, client service, and product development "silo up," if that is the predisposition of the manager and the culture of the organization. It needs to be perfectly clear that the rules are not negotiable. Although we go to great pains not to address it directly, you are *not* running a democracy, even if some very good employees find that view unacceptable.

There is no clear answer as to how to run a business most successfully. Start-ups tend to run with one P&L; everyone is involved in everything, and no one is making any meaningful amount of money. As an organization gets larger, it is more likely to operate functionally: it is more likely to hire specialists; its leader will seek accountability; she will also need to create tools to measure performance. These midsize firms' requirements for accountability and performance measurement are fertile ground for the development of silos. All of these silo issues are part of the larger cultural challenge you must deal with. Crossing the cultural divide is the challenge that never goes away. You will deal with silos on your first day as leader, on every day you serve in that capacity, and on your last day, as you influence the selection of your successor.

Leadership

It is generally accepted in management circles that A players tend to hire A players. It is also well accepted that B players tend to hire C players, as a statement of their own competency concerns. Do you really want a bunch of C players? You must decide how much disruption and mediocrity you are willing to live with as you accept the mantle of leadership. In a perfect world, once a year you should do a full review of the performance and capabilities of each of your senior reports. These are the folks who are running the business, approving the strategies, doing the hiring, and creating the tactics to execute the bold plan that you, as leader, have envisioned. You certainly don't want any B players starting for your team. Not only are they B players, but they will not hire the best people out of fear of being overshadowed. Part of this yearly review should assess their skills to do their jobs and to execute the plan. Have they been promoted beyond their ability to perform?

Annually, or more often, you must also review and determine if your primary strategies are still executable against the goals and vision of the firm. If this sounds daunting, at least you are paying attention.

Change in people and/or direction (which causes more people to be displaced or moved around) is gut wrenching. It is also expensive and disruptive to business and morale. It is, however, required for business survival. Only you, from your vantage point, can determine the optimum speed of these changes. No change at all ensures mediocrity or worse. At the same time, you cannot change everything at once without blowing the place up. To these broad and difficult-to-apply statements, I would add three unequivo-cal observations:

1. If you are going to do a business-related layoff, it is essential that you do it rapidly. Do not drip it out like Chinese water torture. Do it all at once, then communicate to everyone that you are done, and the layoffs are over. Remind your employees that they have your confidence, which is why they are still with the company. Restate the goals and mission of the company and reiterate your high degree of confidence that the new leaner and meaner team is up to the challenge. Stress that, in business, sacrifices are required by some so that the enterprise and its stakeholders may flourish. Then tell them go back to work. Use this as an opportunity to clean house. In the layoff, make sure you include anyone you can't stand, is out to get you, or can't do his or her job.
2. Fire any senior person who is not smart enough to hire well and think strategically. This is your chance to clean out the B players.
3. Eliminate the professional scorpions. It is always the right time to fire a negative, destructive employee.
4. Look at the mules. Have they been marginalized or do they need to go so their area can be looked at and upgraded?

If you think this sounds arbitrary and capricious, you are correct. What's your point? You have a business to run, and you need to reduce the amount of time and energy you invest in people who cannot or will not get on board or who cannot get the job done. You also have to reduce the need to look over your shoulder at who may be gunning for you. Looking over your shoulder increases your wind resistance and just slows you down. It's difficult enough that the competition is always shooting at you and that the economy stinks.

Successful leadership and management can be described as the art of appearing calm on the outside while operating in a constant state of triage on the inside. There is very little room for in-house advice and counsel. If you have a board of directors, the board's job is to protect the outside stakeholders, not you. If you need a place to bounce ideas and test your thinking, one or more mentors, paid or unpaid, official or unofficial, can be extraordinarily helpful.

Simon Sinek, a wonderful business writer who has influenced my approach to business for years, developed the "Golden Circle" for the Rand Foundation. Business is run on what, how, and why. *What* is that which the business is trying to accomplish. The *What* is that which everyone already knows (e.g., make the most money, sell the most cars, have the largest profit margin, be up 10 percent over last year, beat the competition, etc.). *How* represents that which some people know, i.e., the tactics and strategies the firm will employ to achieve the *What*. Examples include proprietary software, a brilliant game plan, a secret source or sauce, a competitive advantage, a new product, a great team, and so forth. *Why* represents what you as the leader know: the reason you do what you do. This articulation is the most difficult. *Why* speaks to the motivation of the enterprise. It speaks to the inspiration that allows employees and customers to experience the power and purpose of the message. Customers and employees want to be part of something larger than themselves.

The *Why* involves messages such as: "to push the envelope," "to expand the event horizon," "the relentless pursuit of perfection" (Lexus), "to change the world," "to perform with precision," and "to deliver the impossible." I am sure that after a couple of drinks, you could come up with dozens. The *Why* is the essence of the enterprise. It is your organization's most prized message. It is the starting point in the communication. Listen to Steve Jobs, the man who, at Apple, engineered one of the most stunning turnarounds in U.S. corporate history. Speaking to the world, at a product rollout introduction, he said: "Everything we do is to challenge the status quo. We approach everything by thinking differently." When Martin Luther King Jr. gave the speech that changed the world, he called it "I Have a Dream"—not "I Have a Plan." A leader's job is to motivate and inspire his or her employees to feel they are part of a grand vision, that they are involved in something larger than themselves. Imparting the actual details of the plan is optional.

SUMMARY

1. Leadership exudes vision as its byproduct.
2. Leaders are invested in outcomes.
3. Leadership is a logical proposition wrapped in an emotional wrapper.
4. Be visible, create a back channel (walking around).

5. It is all about what they hear, not about what you say.
6. Groupthink is your communication tool and your communication challenge.
7. You must get the timing and the message right.
8. Leading is not doing. You lead, everyone else does.
9. Silo management is your greatest challenge and your greatest opportunity.

CHAPTER 3

Persuasion and Negotiation

Welcome to the "sausage manufacturing" chapter of this book. The introduction outlined the elements of this book: a formula on how to manage (chapter 1), including an understanding that success in management creates the need to lead, even though management and leadership are distinctly different activities; a discussion of the elements of effective leadership (chapter 2); and the practical skills, combined with the understanding of the other human beings at the firm, that will allow you to successfully manipulate your environment (chapter 3). This human-centric starting point is the essential element of the model that allows you to create an environment in which your leadership, management skills, and practices will be delivered efficaciously.

Negotiation and persuasion start before a child's first birthday. A child learns when to cry and when to smile to improve his or her environment. As children get older, they develop more tools to expand the scope of their control over their environment, which includes parents, teachers, and friends.

Negotiation, persuasion, and sales are not isolated activities or dirty words. I am treating this topic in this designated chapter, but these activities could just as easily have been discussed as part of each chapter. They are built into everything we do. Businesses engage in one or all of them every day. When you and a friend select a restaurant to eat in or a movie to see, you are engaging in n/p/s on many levels. The movie has advertisements. The restaurant has a website, testimonials, and feedback from friends who have already eaten there. You have predispositions that you bring to the discussion. You love spicy food and love stories; your friend loves action movies and gets heartburn walking past an Indian restaurant. You make deals with your kids, your spouse, your friends, even your travel agent or hairdresser. Life is filled with compromises, and you are constantly negotiating everything you do. Business operates in the same way.

The organized study of persuasion is traced to Aristotle, who wrote *The Rhetoric* in the fourth century BC. Professors still routinely assign this book in college philosophy and communications classes. Interestingly, persuasion is so significant in human interactions that we have been talking about it since the dawn of the written word—or since women needed the protection of men and men started looking for dinner and a little romance. It should be noted that, in the western world, women's roles and needs have evolved rapidly; men, not so much.

There is little written in understandable form that offers a unified theory about understanding and effectively implementing persuasion. That is because n/p/s may be too complex to simplify adequately. We all want the Cliffs Notes version of the centralizing theorem. Some areas of study are complex enough that they defy summarization or conceptualization. Try reading a beginner's manual on quantum physics, focusing on string theory. Trust me, it really is simplified. Yet most readers (this author included) are lost by page six. A model for successful negotiation is difficult to verbalize and even more difficult to execute with a rule-based methodology. Even so, it is important to develop a framework for your approach.

THE NUTS AND BOLTS OF GETTING IT DONE

The list below is the most important advice I can share about negotiation:

1. Operate in the realm of the feasible.
2. Leave your emotions at the door.
3. Nothing important ever happens in the first act.
4. The most important information is what the other side cannot live without.
5. It is essential to remain focused on what *you* cannot live without and to deny that information to your adversary.

In a negotiation, your first goal is to collect information, and the one who is talking is the one who is losing. Ask open-ended questions, and let the other negotiator ramble at length. He is laying out his best arguments before the game has even started. The more he talks, the more you understand about what he wants and needs. This is the most valuable part of the interaction.

As a human being, your most precious resource is time. Once it is squandered, you can never get it back. Some people like to negotiate. It gets their juices flowing; they find the whole activity stimulating. Avoid these people like the plague. They are time wasters and, generally, are not even good negotiators. They do not want to make a deal. They are committed to the game, not the prize for winning it. These people are easy to recognize; their positions keep shifting and their stories keep changing.

Persuasion is a tool, like a hammer or a screwdriver. It is not positive or negative. As a result, everyone, including me, is great at giving entertaining examples of persuasion, but because of the complexity, we are less effective at presenting an all-encompassing approach on how to use it. Human beings are complex creatures. There is no simple explanation for what does and does not work in human interaction. There is no secret formula to predict the effectiveness of one tool over another. That being said, I can shed some light as to what has worked well for me. Work hard to develop a tool kit that works for you—one that is flexible and comprehensive that you can use day in and day out.

The goal in this chapter is to familiarize you with the tool kit available so that you can develop an appreciation of which tools can be used, and under what circumstances. Perhaps even more importantly, I hope to supply you with enough understanding and familiarity to recognize which persuasion tools are being deployed against you in a negotiation. The easiest way to lose a negotiation is not to realize you are playing. There is the old story of the card game with strangers: if you cannot determine quickly who is the sucker in the game, it is because you are the sucker.

At the moment, I am talking in generalities. The terms *negotiation, persuasion,* and *sales* are often confused or used interchangeably. I will try to reserve my use of the word *sales* for external interactions and will do my best to refer to *persuasion* and *negotiation* as tools utilized in external interactions (sales) as well as in the resolution of internal decision-making disputes.

Persuasion pervades our existence; we engage in persuasion as part of our daily existence. Doctors use persuasion (sales) to gain your compliance in taking your medication. They use "I am God—do what I say or something bad will happen," or they co-opt you by giving you explanations you cannot fully comprehend. Try following a doctor as she explains the chemical pathway applications and approaches of beta-blockers versus calcium channel blockers in the management of your high blood pressure. Often, a doctor will treat you as if you should understand this complex information. You do not want to appear like a complete idiot, so you nod your head, which validates the treatment plan.

A skilled doctor or lawyer co-opts you by using his greater knowledge and perspective to get you to do what he wants you to do. He succeeds in manipulating you into viewing yourself as participating in the decision. This is what you want in a doctor or lawyer: someone who listens and who fashions the best possible solution based on your specific issues and concerns. That's what you think your doctor or lawyer is doing. In reality, he is giving everyone in your situation the same—hopefully correct—advice.

These professionals have learned how to persuade you to be their partners by following their generally valid advice. This co-opt approach is a common tool used to gain compliance. It is not bad or good, and it is not just doctors and lawyers who use it. Gaining compliance is what we all want to do; it allows us to control our environment and relationships. It makes us feel safe. Using your greater expertise to convince people that you know materially more than they do about a subject often allows you to co-opt them to your point of view.

This is precisely what happens to me in a computer store with knowledgeable salespeople. First, they make me feel like an idiot by showing me how smart they are. Then they assume (politely lying—they must know I have no idea) that I actually understand what they are talking about. They have accomplished the hard part of the sale. I will likely buy what they tell me to buy. This approach has a weakness: If they fail to convince their target that they are real experts or encounter someone who actually knows more than they do, they are up the creek. Please remember, fear of failure is not a reason to abandon the approach. The goal in sales is to get your share of sales and win the war, not to win every battle.

Persuasion is central to the operation of any business. Persuasion is used in team building, which is an organized way of distilling good ideas. Team building allows the logic of good ideas to be driven by groupthink—an effective approach to persuading the internal participants that in fact these are great ideas, thereby creating ownership. At the opposite extreme, an autocratic leader persuades and creates buy-in with threats and fear. That usually crosses the line from persuasion to intimidation. There is a price to pay for that shortcut. These ideas are under-owned and, therefore, often undermined.

Externally, persuasion is the focus of sales training and sales in general. There is an old saying, "Salespeople are born, not made." Like many old sayings, this one is wrong. Salespeople are, in fact, made, not born. The majority of successful salespeople are created by training, products, marketing, and client support. Very few autocratic, dominant bullies succeed in sales in the modern era.

To be effective at persuasion, a repertoire of responses and tools is required. Use of a variety of techniques cannot be implemented by policy but rather by trial and error, experience, and careful analysis. N/p/s is not like swimming or golf. You cannot get better by yourself. It is more like chess or fencing. Your best teacher is a more skilled practitioner. Success in n/p/s is painful. It often starts with a string of failures. Each attempt is a battle, not a war. You do it, even if you dislike it (everyone hates to lose). It is training for the ever-more-important engagements that lie in front of you as your career unfolds. The outcome of your personal war is not decided until you retire from business and can view the full context of your n/p/s outcomes. Many careers have been built around one or two big wins.

Persuaders employ a variety of techniques. I will try to hit the highlights, but this list is by no means meant to be comprehensive. I urge you to seek some personalized approaches. It is important to realize that this is not a treatise on offensive weapons. Every one of these approaches is just as likely to be used against you as to be utilized by you. To complicate matters even more, these strategies are usually used in combination with one another. It is rare to encounter a one-dimensional approach.

I recently watched the movie *The History of Lying*. It depicted a persuasion-free society. Everybody told the truth about everything. Truth created a wedge between people; no one wanted to hear that every day was a bad hair day. Society was boring and hurtful. The truth drove people apart. I winced when women told men they were unattractive or repulsive. Parents told their kids what they really thought of their art project or their performance in a soccer game.

The contrast between the real world and the movie was striking. It was also instructive as to how integrated persuasion is into the real world. People lie all the time. Often it is innocent: "You look wonderful today. Have you lost weight?" Or polite: "As much as I would like to attend the performance of a medley of experimental dirges performed by your son's junior high school glee club, I have to take care of the funeral arrangements for my hamster, who died last night." The ability to relate drives persuasion. Relating involves staying close and coming across as a genuinely nice person. The truth is often inconsistent with that goal. I recently went shopping with my wife for a new wedding ring in the diamond district in New York. Everyone had a set of lies about the best approach to what she wanted. She ended up buying from the salesperson she liked the best, even though his price was no better or worse than his competitors and his lies no more credible.

Recently, during a short walk on the streets of midtown New York City, I was struck by the sheer number of assaults on my decision-making: homeless people looking helpless; curb cuts to remind me to keep my focus on the handicapped; enticing sale signs and merchandise displayed beautifully in store windows; restaurant menus; branding logos on every car or truck; billboards on buildings and on the sides of buses; political leaflets introducing the next politician who was going to cut taxes, increase services, and reduce the deficit; food smells from the street vendors; music from the clubs; and the solid feel of high-end financial institutions' (if there is such a thing) marble or granite construction, cool to the touch even in the summer. During my short walk, each of my five senses was assaulted. (I tried to come up with an example for "taste," but I was too squeamish to lick anything except for the occasional free food samples in front of a new restaurant.) I did not receive any psychic messages, but I am sure the fortune-teller sitting outside her shop was trying. Take time to observe, even briefly, on a busy street, and you will quickly develop a comprehensive list of your own examples of pitches being targeted at you.

Even your smart phone will point you toward nearby temptations if you download the correct app.

We have talked about co-opting—that is, when the doctor pretends you have a PhD in pharmacology, confuses you in a really complimentary way, and, as a result, gets you to take the blue pill. In chess and in persuasion, if you have not accurately assessed the skill level or knowledge level of your adversary and it turns out he is a better chess player or knows more about the product or service you are purveying than you thought he did, failure will likely result. A skilled chess player will normally defeat an opponent who underestimates him and develops his attack too soon. The person who uses this as his only tool of persuasion subscribes to the philosophy: "If you cannot dazzle them with brilliance, baffle them with bull." It does not represent a comprehensive approach to persuasion. Avoid the temptation to select a single tool as the approach to every situation. Co-opting is most effective when you are sure you have an informational advantage.

We have also talked about bullying. When your superior or your doctor wants you do something and hasn't read my brilliant chapter on management, she may resort to bullying: "Do this or you are fired," or "Take the blue pill or you are going to die." This technique applies only in situations in which you are in total control of the activities of others. It generates significant resentment and is much less effective than you might suspect. A good friend of mine is an endocrinologist and world-class bully. He reports that less than half of his diabetes patients are compliant with their medication, despite his best efforts to scare the hell out of them. In a business environment, direct threatening usually results in an employee observing the letter of what is being requested and ignoring the spirit of the request. It is a poor choice for a manager who is interested in leveraging his outcomes. When bullying is used in any other way, I view it as coercive and, like blackmail, beyond the scope of ethical business practice.

I could write a whole chapter on guilt. After all, I did have a Jewish mother, and therefore I am a qualified expert. Guilt is actually a somewhat effective method of persuasion. It is often combined with exhaustion and affinity, which we will discuss separately. In business, weak persuaders utilize guilt. For the purpose of this discussion, *weak* has two distinct meanings: it relates to individuals who are just not good at persuasion, and it applies to having a weak value proposition. In both cases, guilt will be one of the tools employed in getting someone to make a favorable decision. Guilt is usually associated with time. "He is a really nice guy and has spent so much time and been here so many times; I'll feel bad if we don't give him some business." As I said, guilt is normally utilized in conjunction with other tools from the toolbox. Alone it is a hangdog kind of low-end tool, typically generating subpar results. Do you want them to throw you a bone or give you a side of beef?

Exhaustion is another low-end and not very successful tool when used alone. Keep your targets in your control, make them invest a lot of time, keep talking, and someone may buy your value proposition just to shut you up.

Typically, these are small mercy orders. Your clients agree to something just so you will go away. Clearly, exhaustion has only a small role in persuasion and negotiation, but I am certain you will observe it in your corporate life. In proper combination with other tools, it can be utilized quite effectively.

The bushwhack is the classic ambush. It is a famous and effective persuasion tool. The old story is the guy who calls the girl and says, "Are you free Saturday night?" Happily, she says yes, to which he responds, "Great, I'm moving to a new apartment. Can I count on you to help?" Its application in corporate life is only slightly less subtle. Manager A says to Manager B: "I have a chance to involve another group in a big project we are working on. Do you have any people you could free up on your team to help? This is a big deal, and their contribution would be very visible." That is the bait. Don't bite. Your team will get credit for having so little else to do that they can chip in and perform some menial portion of this project that Manager A didn't want his group burdened with—or Manager A gets credit for getting the project done in record time.

This reminds me of the dialogue between an old Wall Street pro and an up-and-coming trader. The pro asks, "If you're walking down Broad Street in front of the New York Stock Exchange and you see a fifty-dollar bill lying in middle of the sidewalk, what should you do?" The trader isn't sure of the answer, so the old pro tells him, "Cross the street and walk the other way—fast. You don't want to get hit by the safe they are going to drop on the head of the guy who picks up the fifty." Remember, if it sounds too good to be true it probably is. Watch out for these open-ended setups by others, and find ways to use them to your advantage. Look for ways to bring other groups into your projects so you get to look good upstairs.

Affinity, as a tool, is seized upon at the drop of a hat. Anything the persuader can do to make you feel more comfortable and familiar with her helps her in the negotiation process. For example, a persuader using affinity might say, "Oh, you have children in elementary school? So do I." A good persuader is trying to build an affinity bridge from the first moment you meet and will often grasp at any straw: "Oh, you are active in the Presbyterian church? So is my brother's sister-in–law's best friend's mother's dog walker. I hear it is really great." Use it if it is there. Do not reach to make it work.

A better approach might be using other persuasion tools like problem solving with urgency and agitation: "We are here today because we want to get something accomplished (problem solving). It will be challenging to do so because the opportunity is complex and has implications for other decisions you may need to make (agitation). In addition, there is an aggressive timetable (urgency) we both need to meet to make this decision quickly and to have the outcome be efficacious."

Logic is also a powerful tool: "This is the very best season to make this deal because the waiting time is the shortest." Logic is usually delivered with missed opportunity and scarcity. Scarcity and missed opportunity are the modern-day versions of lowballing: "You know we are offering you a great deal; we can only afford to offer it to you until next Tuesday." Or here's another: "We both know we are the best provider of this activity. You might as well take advantage before the offer expires." Or again, "The next deal we sign is the last deal we can do at this price, or in this timeframe, and we are close to signing with several others." (You are not backing yourself in a corner; you can always, as a giant personal concession, agree to the same terms later.)

Another tool you can use to persuade is groupthink and social conformity. Social scientists have demonstrated that the larger the group, the greater the compliance to the dominant idea. Most people who turn sixty-five sign up for Medicare; sometimes, even if it results in less satisfactory medical coverage than they have at their current employer who offers a private more comprehensive medical plan. If your neighbor buys a BMW, your chances of buying one increase. If three neighbors buy one, your chances increase even more. Often, we hear examples like "you'll feel better about yourself," or "it will help you relate to young people." (Translation: That is what the other people of your age and circumstances are agreeing to; it will make you seem cool and help you feel young.) Social conformity can be summed up as "Everyone else is doing it." If this sounds like high school, that's because it *is* like high school. We grow up, but the social influences of adolescence, apparently, stay with us well into adulthood.

Another tool, "foot in the door," is as old as the hills and works as well today as it ever has. Here's what it looks like: "We are calling today to offer you a free vacation in Florida.

There is absolutely no obligation to buy anything." What does this mean? (Remember the fifty-dollar bill?) It means that a real estate developer thinks it is worth two thousand dollars to get to pitch you on buying a vacation home in his Florida development. He gets to put on the full-court press and must have a great closing rate to be able to afford that kind of upfront expense. Car companies pay you to take test drives. Even though it is an expense, they have learned that test drivers are much more likely to become buyers.

Persuasion texts also talk about the tool "door in the face," which involves offering the most expensive product or most expansive service. This is offered with the expectation of getting a quick no in response. That no is the door in the face. It is used to effectively position the midrange product or service as a better value. Robert Cialdini (2000) suggests that the sharp negative response to the first offer sets up a sense of debt or guilt that makes the buyer more disposed to accept the second, more reasonable offer. I personally dislike the approach, but there is ample evidence that it does create an enhanced sales opportunity. We have all asked or been asked for a big raise. Despite the discomfort and risk associated with asking, doing so often sensitizes the employer to consider the value of the employee. Not surprisingly, it typically does result in an above-average increase. Within reason, it seems to be true that the squeaky wheel gets the oil.

Lastly, add the three Cs to your toolbox: creditability, charm, and charisma. Creditability is—primarily but not exclusively—generated by expertise with a measured dose of confidence. Charm has always been elusive for me, but for many it is second nature. I believe charm is driven by presenting yourself as personally connected to the interests of the adversary (my choice of *adversary* as a descriptor likely gives you insight as to my charm challenges.) Charisma is a gift. If you have it, use it. If you do not, go out and get it. Some believe either you have it or you don't. I have observed people grow in their position, increase their confidence level, and become more charismatic. We know from the research that as you improve your body language, the strength of the vocabulary you utilize, the aspiration level of your message, your clothes, your ability to establish and maintain eye contact, and your confidence level, you are perceived as being more charismatic. Many places offer training in becoming a better communicator; commit to getting better!

THE COMPLEX SALE

A classic example of complex persuasion is the car salesperson. She employs a multi-tool sales approach. "Hi there, so you need a new car. Let's see how I can help you." (She is using bushwhack; she assumes you are there to buy.) She will pay you to take a test drive (foot in the door), paying you to acquire you as a sales lead. The goal is to keep you in the showroom as long as humanly possible (exhaustion). If she keeps you long enough, there is no time left to visit other dealers. If there are two buyers shopping together, one is likely to be less interested in the process than the other and will start looking at his watch. First you wait for a salesperson; then you wait for her to find a car you can test drive; then the ritualistic copy the license and fill out the test drive information forms. Then, after the test drive, you must wait to sit down with the salesperson for the debrief.

Most people don't buy a car without a test drive, so all the Internet preparation in the world cannot spare you this torturous process. Now the real sale begins. "I used to drive the car you are driving currently…I know you will love the Blitzer…I live right down the block from you and drive one every day (affinity)…I have sold a ton of these to people in your situation…Everyone loves them. I know you will (groupthink and social conformity)…Have you read the comparisons? Best "fuel injection to braking" ratio in the industry. This car has the highest torque (I defy any-one who is not a mechanical engineer to appreciate the rel-evance of torque) and skid pad outcomes of any minivan manufactured in the United States on Tuesdays west of the Mississippi (co-opting and logic)…There is a special promo-tion this month. If we can sign by Thursday, I can save you real money (urgency)…Candidly, we both know you need to upgrade your transportation. You have spent a lot of time here, thinking about it. Folks like you and me, who are young at heart but sensible, are buying this car in large numbers, and I have only two left. Even so, I can get you a great deal (the consolidated close: everything but the kitchen sink in the wrap up)." I think you get the picture. There is a reason there are more registered cars in the United States than valid driver licenses. There are also a lot of people who own vacation homes that they don't want or need as a result of "free vacations."

You might ask why I am spending an entire chapter on something as unimportant as negotiation. After all, you are an accountant. What does this have to do with you? Everyone trying to build a career in a corporate environment will be repeatedly engaged in negotiation. You negotiate for more responsibility, for more money, for a better office, for a longer vacation, for a date with the guy at the water cooler. You negotiate with your parents, your friends, your spouse, your mistress (or mister), your gardener, your landlord, your boss, your reports, and your competition, both internally and externally. Negotiation may well be the most important survival tool you can develop. I think it is worth the retail value of the book, but I am biased and willing to negotiate.

Someone once said, "When the chicken dances with the elephant, the chicken would be wise to let the elephant lead."

Just remember the most important things when you sit down to deal:

1. How strong is your value proposition?
2. How strong is your political position with your adversary?
3. Are you the chicken or the elephant?

If you have considered these things, you are now ready to negotiate a deal. As a general rule, be on time, come dressed as you expect the other combatants to be dressed, come rested, and do not have an important meeting you must attend any time soon. You never want to break off a negotiation session that is going your way. If things are going poorly, you can always claim to have another meeting in order to retreat and regroup. Do not play silly power games; do not get caught up in the "home court advantage" syndrome (the theory that you emanate more power when you are in your own space). It is not important to create some physical environmental advantage.

The person on the other side is likely experienced; he has seen and heard it all before, so save the home court advantage routine for the rookie league. It is more important to be organized about the issues in your mind. Do not script this; the more energy you waste writing down everything you want to say, the worse you will do in this engagement. If you must bring something into the room, make a list of the points you want to make, in bullet form—that's it. Remember the three Cs. This is where charm, credibility, and charisma do the most good.

Take the high ground. Conventional wisdom about negotiation suggests that you disadvantage yourself by speaking first. Conventional wisdom, as is often the case, is dead wrong. Speaking first allows you to set guidelines that frame the tone and purpose of the meeting. Played properly, the other side will agree to your ground rules. It allows you to reset the tempo or tone of the negotiation at any point if the conversation starts to drift off plan. You are grabbing first mover advantage—or playing white in chess. Effectively, your opposition is willingly handing you an enduring edge in this drama. *Take it!*

A good opening might look like this: "Hi, John. I am really glad we finally arranged this meeting to see if we can find a way to work on this project together (or implement this software, or change this reporting line, etc.)…I view things like this as a collaboration, not a contest or negotiation. I would like to proceed on that basis, and I hope you feel the same way (assuming the order)…I am sure you would agree this can only happen if it works for both of us (here I am personalizing it, empowering the other side to find a way to get something he wants and get a deal done)…Any deal we reach needs to be fair to both sides (saying to him you want to get something, but you accept you have to give up something to get it)…If we can't reach an agreement, then we can shake hands and walk away friends. We can both say we bargained in good faith and maintained our professionalism (or served the common good or acted responsibly to our employers, etc.)…Tell me what is most important to you. Tell me what you cannot live without."

By speaking first, I get to determine where my opponent's areas of greatest concern lie. I also get to state the ground rules, which sound like motherhood and apple pie, while setting me up to bushwhack him later by using what we have mutually agreed upon. The goal in this exercise is to generate an information dump in which he is sharing all of his meaningful issues. That is the mother lode. He is supplying you with a road map to fashion a great deal that works for you. People feel comfortable and in control when they are speaking; use their insecurity to garner a better deal.

Even if one or more of your opponent's concerns is easy, your concession response should be, "I think we can get to that. Let's make sure all the big issues are on the table." What you really mean is, "Let us make sure all *your* big issues are on the table." You may have issues that are important to you but not to him. There is no reason to hand him those bargaining chips. Never concede anything unless you get something in return. You might be indifferent to his biggest concern. If he is willing to concede your must-have issue, you will get something you need in exchange for conceding something you don't really care about. That is an excellent start to the negotiation. We all want the elusive win-win, but a good second choice is the more common "win-lose"—as long as you get the win.

An example might be helpful. A car dealer lets you know that his big issues are price and making the sale today. You have not disclosed your core issues to him. You are price sensitive and you want a four-year lease instead of three at the same rate, but you have no problem making a deal today. Because you are aware of his big issues, you say, "I want a four-year lease, same rate, another thousand dollars off the price, and I am prepared to make a deal right now." You understood his core issues. You gave up nothing of importance and got everything you wanted. You learned that he cared about something you did not care about; you used that information to enhance your outcome.

You have taken control of the meeting; you have his big issues and the rough order of importance he places on them. Objectively, there are terms that must be settled that are not on anybody's list. Find a way to hand him control of the issues that neither you nor he care about. This allows you to focus on the issues that are important to you and settle them easily, without having to concede much ground. Remember, you have never really shared what your must-haves are with him. This is the hard part of this activity (and this chapter). This is the moment in the meeting where behavior gets unpredictable and the road map becomes three dimensional. This is where the most variables are open for discussion. This is where it is too complex to script. This is where you must relax, take a deep breath, speak slowly, and think before you speak. This should be your goal in any negotiation. Unfortunately, negotiations rarely turn out this way. So let us return to earth after this theoretical portrayal of the gold standard in making a deal.

Make your introductory remarks. Then get your opponent to tell you as much as he is willing to tell relating to what he really wants. Tell him what you want in general terms. Keep it short. Try not to communicate your walk-away issues. He may hand you your most important concern without you having to give up much to get it. Sometimes your must-haves are visible to everyone. They will immediately attract the attention of even a novice negotiator on the other side of the table. A good friend of mine recently had this experience. As he approached the end of a long and successful career, he desired to improve the quality of his remaining work years by trading the security of a large company (in order to get rid of the rules and constraints of working for a large company) for a smaller, more personal, less bureaucratic environment.

He transferred his client base to a new firm, giving up his present income for a shot at an even greater income somewhere down the road. Even more important to him was the creation of a work environment that would be more to his liking. He and his younger partners signed an airtight agreement to share the revenues equally, even though they all recognized that my friend was doing more to establish the business, whereas the younger partners were expected to be the primary builders of the revenue base. Within months of the establishment of this business, the younger partners realized that my friend didn't really need the money (that, of course, is crazy; almost everyone thinks they need money, but that is for a different book). They came to understand that lifestyle and environment were of utmost importance to him. Recognizing that—and being greedy and unscrupulous—the younger partners immediately started reframing the deal to give my friend less and less of the money he was supposed to get, simply because they knew that lifestyle was important to him and that he was unlikely to try, at his age, to take his clients and start over somewhere else.

We see this in the legal profession all the time. Many lawyers who have worked long hours their entire career are simply emotionally unable to stop working. This does not stop their law firms from forcing them out as partners and having them work "of counsel," which means they are not really participating in the revenues of the firm. They do get a place to go, some stuff to work on, and some percentage of any business they bring to the firm. We have not really evolved very far—even your lifelong business partners will often sell you down the river if they believe they can get away with it. I repeat: do not go running to disclose your real must-haves!

The most effective way to get a satisfactory outcome is to present a compelling argument that your approach is the best, fairest, or easiest. To do that, it is not sufficiently compelling to present a logical case. Studies suggest that two-sided refutational messaging is the most convincing presentation methodology. We all have experienced this in political debates. Generally, each side presents their sound bites, and pundits argue about who won a close debate. In other words, no one looks good or bad; no voters' minds are changed. These exchanges are not really debates—just a series of short speeches. In our society, with our lowered expectations, we take some comfort in observing that, with coaching, many of our future elected officials are smart enough to walk and chew gum simultaneously—at least on some subset of topics.

The real wins and losses come when someone has screwed up—made a factual error or presented a logical inconsistency that is observed and pointed out by the opposition for all to observe. To be most effective, it is not enough to state your opinion. You must also demonstrate the errors in logic or facts of your opponent's argument—hence, the need to refute effectively the views of the other side in this negotiation. The gold standard is being able to point out examples of times when the approach they are presenting has failed in the past. Often, you know what the other side's issue is going to be; a little mental preparation may go a long way. On the other hand, sometimes you just have to go into the meeting blind.

Listen! Much of the important information in a negotiation is between the lines. After the initial exchange of information, usually the one who listens the best wins and the one who talks the most loses. Relax. Do not let your discussion digress into an argument; don't feel the need to respond to everything being said or proposed. Your silence makes the other side uncomfortable. Often she will rebid her original offer simply because you did not respond. I love it when people negotiate with themselves; it makes life much easier and improves the outcomes. Acknowledge her statement but do not run to add new information or revised terms. This is where you may have to adjust your dialogue on the fly. This is why you have been listening so closely. Your adversary, who is nervous and talking too much, is likely supplying you the information you need to control the situation; your first-mover advantage is still running your way. If she gives you a powerful new argument to use, add it to your short list of strong points. If she anticipates and responds to an argument you were considering making, leave it on your short list. It means she is concerned enough about its veracity that she wants to discourage you from verbalizing it.

Stick with your strongest points (this is your short list). If you have logical, compelling arguments, do not be afraid to reframe them and repeat them until he responds. If he has read this book, and you are making a good argument, he will try to ignore it. Do not let him get away with it; ask him to respond to your "killer" point directly. Bring him back to your point when he wanders and tries to make unrelated points in order to change the subject. You need to stay on message and avoid the temptation to weaken a strong point just because he is not responding to it. Your opponent is uncomfortable when you do not respond; be aware of that and guard against becoming uncomfortable when he doesn't respond.

He is not responding because he knows it is a good point and he doesn't have a good answer. In that situation, push him on the winning point. It is actually possible to be the good cop and the bad cop simultaneously; that is what the setup at the beginning of this chapter was all about. "Listen, Joe, we agreed in the beginning that we were going to approach this negotiation in a professional way and at the end either shake hands and walk away or make a deal. I plan to live up to that agreement (good cop). On the other hand, I have given you the reasons I believe my approach is the fairest (or safest or cleanest, etc.). I think you owe it to me and to the spirit of our agreement to respond to my point (bad cop)." He can run, but he cannot hide.

Keep it short, and keep it general. Many more negotiations fall apart in discussions of the small details than in discussions of the broad precepts of the deal. We have all heard the expression "The devil is in the details." As with many common expressions, this one is largely incorrect. The "devil" is in the small-minded people who would rather pick a fight than make a deal. As mentioned earlier, try not to focus on the minor aspects, and try to avoid dealing with people who do. Settle the major points first. If you reach agreement on the major points and you still want the deal on those terms, reach across the table, shake hands, and say, "I am so glad we have been able to reach an agreement in principal (assume the order). We have agreed on all the main points. I am sure we can work out the details." (Or better yet, "Let's get the lawyers to write it up" or "Let's have the staff folks dot the i's and cross the t's,") Declare victory; do not keep talking after you have gotten the order. You are more likely to talk yourself out of an agreement than to improve one by more talk on the topic. If you must keep talking, I suggest the weather, baseball, or shoes.

Agree, as a first step, on your actual top-line goals. For example, "I want an efficient way to upgrade my transportation," not "I want to buy a car at a low price, and you want to sell me one at a high price." Price is only one of many metrics. It is not the top-line goal. Another example might be, "Our goal should be to have you become more productive so you can make more money," not "You want a raise, and I think you are already overpaid for your contribution" (you lazy sloth).

Do not enter negotiations with any mythological predispositions. There is no one correct answer, just an infinite set of potential solutions. You may be able to identify the optimal solution for your side, but that is unlikely to be the final solution. The other side has to perceive it has received something in return. There are the rare win-wins—we should seek them but should not expect to find them very often in a business setting. You may be surprised to find that people do, occasionally, think outside the box. Something may be put on the table that you had not anticipated. Do not reject it out of hand. If it is important enough, break the meeting (you just remembered that "floating" next meeting we discussed earlier) to think it through. There is often more than one way to solve a puzzle; keep your mind open and your mouth shut. Make your opponent pay for any and every no answer. "OK, that concession doesn't work for you. What will you give up?" This would be a great place to introduce your secret must-have—dressed up as a barely acceptable, not that important, second choice.

There are three great errors in negotiation: The first is disclosing your must-haves upfront. The other two are making Type A errors or Type B errors. These concepts are derived from the study of statistics. Type A errors represent the likelihood of deciding (incorrectly) that something that is in fact true, is false. The more subtle is the Type B error, which is the likelihood of deciding (incorrectly) that something that is, in fact, false is actually true. I apologize if that explanation lacks full clarity (I completed my MBA when dinosaurs walked the earth. My final project was run on punch cards and printed on papyrus.) It is easier to understand these errors in a business application. Type A errors are errors in which you assume that you are smarter than you are. These generally pass with time and experience; making enough stupid mistakes in your early working years will usually produce some level of humility. Based on my experience, Type B errors are more subtle and more resistive to modification. They are errors in which you assume that someone else (invariably the person you are negotiating with) is dumber than she actually is. Each of these common errors can be fatal to a negotiation. Making Type A errors usually passes with time and experience, but there is a stubborn resistance to giving up the notion that the person negotiating with you is an idiot. Get over it.

Negotiating is not about winning or losing in the typical sense. It is about getting the best deal you can with the hand you are dealt. Making a deal or reaching an agreement is winning. Reaching an agreement is the prize you are paid for. As in all things corporate, grab the moral high ground. It is about collaboration, communication, and cooperation. Negotiation is always a compromise; leave your persona at home. It doesn't matter if you are winsome and seductive, an alpha male, or any of the gender gradations in between. Save that stuff for sales. Winning is getting a fair deal based on the position of the pieces on the board and the talent of the person you are playing against. The choice of the persuasion tools you use should vary depending on the gender, value proposition, experience, and predispositions of the players.

A study published by Paolo Carli in 2004 suggests that men are more persuasive than women—not because of their ability but because of the perceptions of the people being persuaded. Both men and women tend to view men as more competent. The same study also suggests that women are more easily persuaded than their male counterparts. Carli's study implies that women suffer more profoundly from negative gender bias in their perceptions of men and women in business. These gender stereotypes cause people to believe that men are more competent; in turn, they expect women to be warmer, less competitive, and more nurturing than men. The study suggests that both men and women share these stereotypical views.

This creates a nearly impossible situation for women. Based upon these findings, they must present more competently than their male counterparts in order to be perceived as equally competent. Yet women are usually perceived more negatively than their male counterparts when they are direct, assertive, and forceful. So if a woman presents as competent, she is perceived as less likeable and she damages her ability to create a strong affinity with the person she is trying to persuade, irrespective of her target's gender. Women are playing on an uneven and unfair playing field because of these longstanding gender biases. The successful woman finds a way. It is usually customized to her specific skills, and that customization is often her greatest strength. Women start at a disadvantage, but my experience is that as a result they are often more creative, work harder, and are more unpredictable in their approach.

Therefore, the smart and successful female persuaders you encounter should not be expected to use typical male tools, deployed with traditional or recognizable methodology, in their persuasion approaches. They must adapt, take advantage of societal biases, and turn them to their advantage. That means they represent a special challenge for you. Successful women will have a more comprehensive and flexible tool kit. Their approach may be more emotional and collaborative compared to the straightforward charge of the rooster. Women trying to persuade men or other women will use their most effective weapons. This is, by no means, a criticism of women or a knock on their skills. In fact, the opposite is true. My belief and experience is that women, adjusted for all variables, are usually better employees than their male counterparts. They work harder, work better in teams, have greater flexibility, and have more realistic expectations associated with anticipated outcomes.

Every successful person develops a customized toolkit based on what is comfortable and works most effectively for him. Because of this variety, there is no dependable way to predict your adversary's approach. The aim of this book is to help you recognize what is going on when you see it. Analyze it and respond effectively. I am also trying to get you to relax and amend your approach based on what you observe. If you have a plan and are unwilling to modify your plan based on the responses you receive, you will most likely be unhappy with the result.

Other factors also influence the methodology of persuasion you should utilize. Upon entering a negotiation, it is incumbent on you to understand the nature of the adversary. In an external negotiation, observations you make during your first meeting may be critical in determining the approach you should expect. Often people will tell you how to sell them and what to sell them simply by asking. You might say, "The last thing I would want to do, Ms. Jones, is waste your valuable time. What size Widgets are you configured to use? What time of the year do you typically order?"

If this is an internal negotiation, is the other side a superior, a counterpart, or a direct report? It does not take a management book to help you realize you have more limited positive outcome expectations when dealing with superiors than you do in dealing with counterparts or reports. That being said, when negotiating with your superior, hold onto the general themes of communication with superiors that we have discussed in this book. When you want your superior to agree to your request, don't forget to frame it properly: "As I have communicated many times, Ms. Boss, I know the only way I can advance my career is by making you look good. This plan, for the following reasons, is focused on that outcome." Working in business is like working for a corrupt (but generally unarmed) dictator: his demands on your behavior center largely on making him look good or helping him feel more comfortable. Remember that and you will be a better negotiator.

Who else will you run into at the negotiation table?

If your opponent is a rooster, winning is everything and he doesn't much care how he does it. Approach roosters the way we discussed earlier: set the ground rules and let them tell you their definition of winning: "What would be a win for you?" The good thing about roosters is that they value time. They are willing to over-disclose to get on with the deal. They rarely have the patience to deal with the nuances of disclosure. If they agree to give you your must-haves, you can use their must-haves to convince them they have won: "It's a great deal for your side." Remember, winning has only two definitions: getting a deal you can live with and walking away from a deal you cannot live with. Winning is not a negotiation point…except to young roosters.

Play them: "I will give you the three-year deal that you need in exchange for exclusive distribution rights, a travel and promotional budget, and half the profit." Roosters will give away too much to get their prize. Once you have figured out what they need to win, restructure the rest of the deal to your advantage. Roosters are also the guiltiest of Type B errors (assuming incorrectly that others are not smart). Fashion a deal you can live with and play jujitsu with him; use the single-mindedness of his charge to outflank him. Let him win the battle he is focused on and lose the war he is fighting.

The mule is harder. Typically, mules will be counterparts or reports. They are virtually never external negotiators. (What company would select someone who is systematically opposed to change as a negotiator?) Their superiors have long since learned that negotiation requires flexibility and the ability to compromise, qualities that mules simply do not have. If this is an internal negotiation, the mule's position is perfectly predictable: "Everything I do works perfectly, and any change would cost money, create a disruption, create a business risk, and be more expensive to maintain." What they are really saying is: "It is uncomfortable for me to accept change. Any attempt by you to create it is a personal insult to what I have done. It is also a threat to my control because then others would know how to do what I do."

Negotiating with a mule is a challenge, because you need the mule's help. Mules live in a self-defined world. In many cases, they are the only ones who really know how a particular system works currently. If you want to drive the process, either you need to give them their must-have, a sense of control and feeling of safety, or you can give them a "smack in the head with a two-by-four." Played properly, I believe you can deliver both. Here is an example: "I and your boss (always close the back door) have discussed your area of responsibility. We believe that it should be discontinued entirely, and the responsibilities distributed to their functional areas (translation: we are trashing your silo and assigning the parts to other silos), or it should be expanded under competent leadership (maybe you) into a larger, more comprehensive unit within the firm. Those are really the only two choices from our perspective. You may see it differently, but the unit is too small to offer the career opportunity we think our senior employees should have. Which way do you think we should go? We would like you to lay out a detailed plan." In my experience, if you just ask for the plan you will get an endless argument and never get a comprehensive plan. If he realizes he is a "dead man walking" without it, you will be amazed how quickly the mule can be motivated.

Turtles don't negotiate, and scorpions cannot be negotiated with. You cannot make a deal with someone who is always in search of the lose-lose. You will find yourself negotiating with the RITR—the rock in the road. An RITR, or an armadillo (because they are always blocking the road), is a combination of a turtle, an organization freak (which you always need), and a "glass is half-empty" person. She is the person at the meeting who is always seeing insurmountable obstacles on the path (hence, rocks in the road). Internally, it is common to find yourself in negotiation with an RITR. These folks are often the spine of an organization. They are smart and tenacious. They are in your way because they believe there are problems and unforeseen challenges with your plan. They are the ones who prevent "ready, fire, aim" syndrome. The roosters try to drag the decision-making and implementation along at breakneck speed. The RITRs frustrate the roosters by trying to convince them that the obstacles to success are insurmountable. RITRs are not mules; they see the big picture and want change and good outcomes. They also work hard and stay focused on the mission. They pay attention to the details of what can go wrong or be missed. They are often the project managers within the organization. They will drive a rooster crazy, but often they will end up saving the rooster's hide.

Negotiating with an RITR is an entirely different experience. She is perfectly willing, even anxious, to lay out the rocks. The path to winning here is to deal with each rock systematically. With RITRs, there is no magic rock. Each rock is a deal killer for them. RITRs are not creative problem solvers. They are tenacious problem identifiers, detailed and organized cataloguers, and solution implementers. They do not usually agree or disagree with your plan. They are just afraid it cannot be implemented and that they will be blamed, or that the organization will suffer. A successful negotiation generally consists of discussing each obstacle and satisfying the RITR that there is a satisfactory solution. The busy manager is often frustrated by the tedious nature of this process. On the other hand, completing the rock removal process demanded by any RITR worth his salt often becomes the final vetting process for the planned corporate change and, therefore, is well worth the time and effort.

In any negotiation, it is essential that you honestly evaluate the strength of your hand. Do you have a winner's hand? If you do, you should expect a winner's outcome. The negotiated agreement should reflect the views you had going into this negotiation. You should leave the other side a scrap of clothing to go home with, but you have less need to be flexible or make meaningful concessions. A winner's hand is generated, externally, by excellent cost-effective products, specialized expertise, or a unique cost-saving opportunity. Internally, a win can be generated by a superior position in the negotiation, a stronger set of cost-effective arguments, or a decision-maker in your pocket ("the fix is in"). Everyone likes to negotiate from a position of strength. Unfortunately, you generally do not get the chance. You also don't need my help to do it effectively.

This chapter was written with the assumption that negotiation is occurring on a relatively even playing field, where your hand is roughly as strong as the other party's.

We have talked about tactics to achieve a marginally to materially better outcome than the strength of your hand would have predicted. Sometimes, you find yourself negotiating from a weak position. When Sun Tzu wrote the *Art of War* 2,400 years ago, he was clear about what to do: "If your enemy is superior in strength, evade him." He believed strongly that you should not fight a battle you are not likely to win. In modern corporate life, sometimes you have no choice. So even if your products are mundane, you have no specialized expertise or cost-saving argument, you are the weaker party, your arguments are second-rate, and you have no decision-maker winking at you, many times you still must play the game.

Short-term outcomes in these circumstances are likely to be muted. That is corporate speak for "you are going to get a deal crammed down your throat." Think long and hard; is there any way to avoid negotiating at this time? If this is a good sales lead, can you save it for the next opportunity when your product or service cycle is in your favor? Often, you are not in control. Approach it realistically, focus your efforts on long-term outcomes, and build bridges to the future by the professionalism you demonstrate. Try to create a positive path. Use the loss as a way to gain insight as to what went wrong. What mistakes did you make? Collect information about how the winner set up her value proposition to prevail. Plant the seeds for your future success. Do not attempt some long-shot outcome that reflects poorly on you or your organization; that is like taking a kill shot that doesn't work. At the very least, stay in the game. Corporate success, like life, is measured by the long-term outcomes. Everyone has a reasonable number of unsatisfactory outcomes. Everyone also thinks that unsatisfactory outcomes are more damaging then they really are.

Everything is negotiable. The more someone says it is not negotiable, the more clearly he is saying, "I don't want to negotiate on this topic." The more strongly he feels the need to avoid a topic, the larger the concession you can extract for not pushing that point. The other side must pay to get what is really important to him. The more certain you are of what is essential to him, the stronger your bargaining position and the greater his payment. Ask yourself, "Do I know, with reasonable certainty, what the other side cannot live without?" Keep to yourself what is important to you. The less the other side knows about how important something is, the less you must concede to get it. Charge a lot for what he wants. Pay as little as possible for what you want.

Remember, this is a process, not an event. It is fine to keep score, but the expectation must be to win your share and to succeed at the negotiations that are important to you or to your goals. It is not essential that you win every interaction. In fact, you may be better served by "throwing back the little ones" to set up for the big, high-value career-maker down the road.

Conclusion

As I said in the introduction, management and leadership are not for everyone. You may have surmised from my intermittent cynicism that management is not my first language; I grew up in a sales environment. Management and then leadership were thrust upon me after twelve years in sales and sales management. Odd as it may seem, I believe my background makes me uniquely qualified to write this book and communicate what I have learned. I love much of what is involved in leadership, and it did come naturally to me. Management, on the other hand, was a meaningful adjustment. Many aspects of management are not on the top of my hit parade. I hate confrontation, and I hate dealing with mules. I, like you, have to decide what an ideal work environment is. Even after you have decided, there is no certainty that you can create it even if you are the boss.

The challenge for us management-leadership types is getting comfortable with the actual responsibility that we accept. We must, fairly, serve the needs of a mixed group of stakeholders. For some of them (the employees), the need is to create a fair balance between the demands of work and home. For the equity stakeholders, you must run a business in as close to an optimal fashion as possible, as it must relate to profitability. There may be times when these efforts seem incompatible with one another. To create a fair work environment, you may need to take the long view on profitability. This plan only works if the equity stakeholders continue to be willing to employ you based on whatever impact your efforts have on your short-term profitability outcomes.

Hiring creates another set of opportunities. The world has changed inexplicably. We are living in a time when finding a good job is harder and more competitive than ever before. Yet the current crop of new employees is more demanding and less committed to work than the generations before them. It is counter intuitive as to why this should be, but it still offers an information advantage to the hiring manager. The sense of entitlement embedded in these young people also creates a meaningful amount of information relating to the strengths and weaknesses of these prospective employees. They want to tell you what they are good at and what kind of environment they want to work in. Compare that to a fifty-year-old professional who has been unemployed for two years. He will present himself as liking everything and good at everything.

To be successful you must occasionally make leaps of faith and pay some attention to honoring industry-specific paradigms, but those are the small parts of success. The key differentiators between success and failure as a manager and a leader are intellectual honesty and stark humility.

The honest part is understanding that all businesses are largely the same. This means the challenges are the same and the opportunities are very similar. Most importantly, the questions you need answered are essentially the same, and the inputs you need to answer those questions are very similar. This is why companies hire consultants. The consulting companies have broken the code. They have a secret list of questions they ask to collect a secret list of information that they want. They magically present their findings with special signature graphics that allow the buyer to see the work and understand the conclusions. The consultants have an uncompromising commitment to get the information they really need—not the information the employees want to supply. Their approach is typically four-pronged:

1. Fully allocate every dollar of cost to some revenue-based activity. There is no such thing as "corporate overhead."
2. Ruthlessly evaluate each external activity relating to positioning, competitive advantages, and market share.
3. For each internal activity, benchmark your fully allocated costs to industry costs as a function of revenue.
4. Present a model that attempts to predict the future growth rate of each external activity.

I strongly suggest you take this approach. If you know the secret questions and how to answer them, you can do the work internally; if you do not know the questions and how to answer them, then you had better hire a consulting firm quickly. The greatest challenge to internal consultancy is getting the employees to cooperate and tell the truth. Smart employees will quickly see the career risk of a fully loaded honest assessment of the bottom-line outcomes of their activities. In almost every organization, a black hole of expenses reduces overall profitability but doesn't affect the individual business unit's outcomes. This is an example of magic silo thinking.

View your organization as an organism. We have spent the bulk of this book trying to predict and manipulate the behavior of individuals, and we have already come to expect limited success in facilitating changes person by person. Contrary to intuition, the behavior of a group of people is easier to predict than a single individual's behavior. There are hundreds of examples of this—from Adolf Hitler to Gandhi. Isaac Asimov, perhaps the world's greatest science fiction writer, in his defining work *The Foundation,* predicted the development of psychohistory, which is the study of the prediction and control of the behavior of large groups in response to defined stimulus. We are certainly seeing modern politics pushing the envelope on this "science."

Management books generally come in two forms: the textbooks that focus on complex management theories that are hard to apply to real-world challenges, and books like this that say, "Trust me, this is the way to do it. I did it this way, and it worked for me." What I have outlined in this book is what I have learned over a forty-year career. It has worked for me, and I do believe it has value in helping you become a better manager and better leader.